RESTAVEC

From Haitian Slave Child

RESTAVEC

to Middle-Class American

JEAN-ROBERT CADET

University of Texas Press
Austin

Tenth paperback printing, 2010

Requests for permission to reproduce material
from this work should be sent to:

Permissions
University of Texas Press
P.O. Box 7819
Austin, TX 78713-7819
www.utexas.edu/utpress/about/bpermission.html

∞The paper used in this book meets the minimum requirements
of ANSI/NISO Z39.48-1992 (R1997) (Permanence of Paper).

Library of Congress Cataloging-in-Publication Data

Cadet, Jean-Robert, 1955–
Restavec : from Haitian slave child to middle-class American
/ by Jean-Robert Cadet.—1st ed.
p. cm.
ISBN 978-0-292-71203-4 (pbk. : alk. paper)
1. Cadet, Jean-Robert, 1955– 2. Haitian Americans—Biography.
3. Children—Haiti—Social conditions. 4. Haiti—Social conditions.
5. Cincinnati (Ohio)—Biography. I. Title.

E184.H27C34   1998
973'.049697294 – dc21
[B]   97-4832

To the memory of my mother,
Henrilia Brutus,

and to my best friend and wife,
Cindy

FOREWORD

My days and nights reverberate with the truth of this story that my husband has written. I was not there to witness the circumstances of his birth, the horrors of his childhood, or his surreal assimilation into American society that form the basis of this memoir, but I lie beside him now each night as he sleeps. And when that sleep is fitful—when I hear his laboring breath, his muffled cry, or feel his arms tremble and his legs thrash about—I know that the reality from decades ago is upon us again.

My mornings greet me with another truth: our son. I know that the combination of my white skin and my husband's brown skin could have created our lovely, beige-skinned boy only through the echoing effects of genes, the genes of "Blanc Philippe," my husband's father. My husband tells me that our son is his reason for writing this, his source of strength. I smile. This is indeed a tale of strength: incredible, forged-in-fire, life-seeking strength. May it be an inspiration to the reader's own days and nights.

Cynthia Nassano Cadet

In 1994, the United States sent in troops to restore democracy in Haiti and to give hope to a people who are accustomed to living under the iron fist of dictators. Yet there are over 250,000 restavecs in Haiti—slave children who have no hope of ever becoming educated participants in the restored democracy. Having lost my own childhood in restavec servitude, I hate knowing that other children are losing theirs the same way.

May this account of my life inspire nations to protect all their children.

J.-R. C.

Note to the Reader: All of the stories told in this book are true, but most of the names have been changed.

1   **"A blanc** [white person] is coming to visit today. He's your papa, but when you see him don't call him papa. Say 'Bonjour, monsieur' and disappear. If the neighbors ask you who he was, you tell them that you don't know. He is such a good man, we have to protect his reputation. That's what happens when men of good character have children with dogs," said Florence to me in Creole when I was about seven or eight years old. Before noon, a small black car pulled into the driveway and a white man got out of it. As I made eye contact with him, he waved at me and quickly stepped up to the front door before I had a chance to say "Bonjour, monsieur." Florence let him in the house and I disappeared into the backyard. Almost immediately I heard him leaving.

At the age of five I had begun to hate Florence. "I wish your maman was my maman too," I told Eric, a little boy my age who lived next door. One day while we played together, Eric's mother pulled a handkerchief from her bra, wet its corner on her tongue, knelt down on one knee, and wiped a dirty spot on her son's face. Eric pushed her hand away.

"Ah, Maman, stop it," he said.

I looked at her with bright eyes. "Do it to me instead," I said.

She stared at my face for a moment and replied with an affectionate smile, "But your face is not dirty."

To which I answered, "I don't care. Do it to me anyway." She gently wiped a spot on my face, as I grinned from ear to ear.

My biological mother had died before her image was ever etched in my mind. I cannot remember the time when I was brought to Florence, the woman I called Maman. She was a beautiful Negress with a dark-brown complexion and a majestic presence. She had

no jobs but earned a small income from tenants who leased her in-
herited farmland. She also entertained high government officials as
a means to supplement her income. Her teenage son, Denis, was
living with his paternal grandmother and attending private school.
Florence claimed that her husband had died when her son was ten
years old, but I never saw her wedding pictures.

I came into Florence's life one day when Philippe, her white former lover, paid her a surprise visit. He was a successful exporter of
coffee and chocolate to the United States and Europe. Philippe lived
in Port-au-Prince, Haiti, with his parents, two brothers, and a niece.
He arrived in his Jeep at Florence's two-story French country-
style house in an upper-class section of the city. A bright-eyed, fat-
cheeked, light-skinned black baby boy was in the back seat.
Philippe parked the car, reached in the back seat, and took the baby
out. He stood him on the ground and the baby toddled off. I was
that toddler.

Philippe greeted Florence with a kiss on each cheek while she
stared at the toddler. "Whose baby is this?" she asked, knowing the
answer to her question.

"His mother died and I can't take him home to my parents. I'd
like you to have him," said Philippe, handing Florence an envelope
containing money.

"I understand," she said, taking the envelope. He embraced her
again and drove off, leaving me behind. Philippe's problem was
solved.

My mother had been a worker in one of Philippe's coffee factories below the Cahos Mountains of the Artibonite Valley. Like the
grands blancs of the distant past who acknowledged their blood in
the veins of their slave children by emancipating and educating
them, Philippe was following tradition. Perhaps he thought that
Florence would give me a better life.

"Angella!" yelled Florence.

"Oui, Madame," answered the cook, approaching Florence.

"Take care of this little boy, will you? Find him something to
eat," she instructed. Angella picked me up.

"What's his name?" she asked.

Florence thought for a moment and said, "Bobby." Florence did
not want another child, but the financial arrangement she had with

Philippe was too attractive for her to turn down. Every night I slept on a pile of rags in a corner of Florence's bedroom, like a house cat, until I was six years old. Then she made me sleep under the kitchen table.

Florence did not take care of me. From the time I entered the household, various cooks met my basic needs, which freed Florence from having to deal with me. I was never greatly attached to any of the cooks, since none of them ever lasted for more than a year. Florence would fire them for burning a meal or for short-changing her when they returned from the market.

As I got older, I learned what kind of day I was going to have based on Florence's mood and tone of voice. When she was cheerful, the four-strip leather whip, called a *martinet*, would stay hung on its hook against the kitchen wall.

I knew three groups of children in Port-au-Prince: the elite, the very poor, and the *restavecs*, or slave children.

Children of the elite are often recognized by their light skin and the fine quality of their clothes. They are encouraged by their parents to speak proper French instead of Creole, the language of the masses. They live in comfortable homes with detached servants' quarters and tropical gardens. Their weekly spending allowance far exceeds the monthly salary of their maids. They are addressed by the maids with "Monsieur" or "Mademoiselle" before their first names. They are chauffeured to the best private schools and people call them "'ti' [petit] bourgeois."

Children of the poor often have very dark skin. They appear dusty and malnourished. In their one-room homes covered with rusted sheet metal, there is no running water or electricity. Their meals of red beans, cornmeal, and yams are cooked under clouds of smoke spewed by stoves made of three coconut-size stones and fueled by dried twigs and wood. They eat from calabash bowls with their fingers and drink from tin cans with sharp edges, sitting on logs while being bothered by flies. They squat in the under-brush and wipe with rocks or leaves. At night, they sleep on straw mats or cardboard over dirt floors while bloodsucking bedbugs feast on their sweaty flesh. They walk several miles to ill-equipped public schools, where they depend on lunches of powdered milk, donated by foreign countries that once depended on the slave labor of their ancestors. After school, they rush home to recite their lessons loudly in cadence before the Caribbean daylight fades away, or they walk a few miles to Park Champ-de-Mars and sit under streetlamps to do their homework while moths zigzag above their heads.

Restavecs are slave children who belong to well-to-do families. They receive no pay and are kept out of school. Since the emancipation and independence of 1804, affluent blacks and mulattoes have reintroduced slavery by using children of the very poor as house servants. They promise poor families in faraway villages who have too many mouths to feed a better life for their children. Once acquired, these children lose all contact with their families and, like the slaves of the past, are sometimes given new names for the sake of convenience. The affluent disguise their evil deeds with the label *restavec*, a French term that means "staying with." Other children taunt them with the term because they are often seen in the streets running errands barefoot and dressed in dirty rags.

Restavecs are treated worse than slaves, because they don't cost anything and their supply seems inexhaustible. They do the jobs that the hired domestics, or *bonnes*, will not do and are made to sleep on cardboard, either under the kitchen table or outside on the front porch. For any minor infraction they are severely whipped with the cowhide that is still being made exclusively for that very purpose. And, like the African slaves of the past, they often cook their own meals, which are comprised of inferior cornmeal and a few heads of dried herring. Girls are usually worse off, because they are sometimes used as concubines for the teenage sons of their "owners." And if they become pregnant, they are thrown into the streets like garbage. At maturity, restavecs are released into the streets to earn their living as shoeshine boys, gardeners, or prostitutes.

I was a restavec in the making. Raising me as such was more convenient for Florence, because then she didn't have to explain to anyone who I was or where I came from. As a restavec, I could not interact with Florence on a personal level; I could not talk to her about my needs. In fact, I could not speak until spoken to, except to give her messages third parties had left with me. I also did not dare smile or laugh in her presence, as this would have been considered disrespectful—I was not her son but her restavec.

My tin cup, aluminum plate, and spoon were kept separate from the regular tableware. My clothes were rags and neighborhood children shouted "restavec" whenever they saw me in the streets. I always felt hurt and deeply embarrassed, because to me the word meant motherless and unwanted. When visitors came and saw me in the yard, I was always asked, "'Ti' garçon [little boy], where is your grown-up?" Had I been wearing decent clothes and shoes, the question would have been, "'Ti' monsieur [young gentleman], where is your mother or father?"

Every night in my bedding under the kitchen table, I wished that either I or Florence would never wake up again. I wanted to live in the world of dreams where I sometimes flew like a bird and swam like a fish. But in the dreamworld I always stopped to relieve myself against a tree, causing me to awake in a hot puddle of urine.

Returning to the real world was a nightmare in itself—I was always trying to avoid Florence, the woman I called maman. Every day I wished Florence would die in her sleep—until I made a most frightening discovery. While cleaning the bathroom one early evening, I noticed a small canvas bag tied into a ball under the sink. Curious, I opened it and found several pieces of blood-stained rags. Suddenly my heart raced, and I became convinced that Florence *was* going to die. I had a strong desire to ask her where the blood came from, but I couldn't. I was allowed to speak to Florence only when she questioned me or when I had to deliver a message from a third party.

The thought of Florence's dying was real in my mind. Sometimes I sobbed, asking God to take back my wish for her death. I began to watch Florence closely, staring at every exposed part of her body, trying to find the source of the blood. I spied on her through keyholes whenever she was in the bathroom or in her bedroom.

One hot and muggy afternoon, after she pinched and pulled me by the skin of my stomach because I had forgotten to clean the kitchen floor, she gave me a small bag of laundry detergent, labeled Fab, and a bottle of Clorox bleach. "Go in the bathroom and wash the rags in the bucket," she commanded with rage. I uncovered the metal bucket and saw a foul-smelling pile of white rags soaking in bloody water. I reached in the bucket and scrubbed each piece until the stains began to fade. I vomited in the toilet and continued with my new chore.

After a small eternity, Florence opened the door. Fresh air rushed in and I filled my lungs. My ragged shirt was soaked with sweat. I looked up and realized for the first time that Florence was the tallest woman I had ever known. After she inspected the rags, she said, "Now soak them in the bleach. Tomorrow you can rinse them." As I followed her instructions, I stared at her feet, searching again for the source of the blood.

The following day, without being told, I scrubbed the rags again, one by one, and rinsed each piece. As I hung them to dry over the clothesline in the backyard, Florence came out to observe. "After they're dry, fold them and put them in this," she said as she handed me the small white canvas bag. I took it from her, scanning her arms and legs for scars. She had none.

I replied, "Oui," instead of the usual "Oui, Maman." At the end of the day, I followed her instructions and placed the bag on her bed. From then on, every month Florence handed me the small white canvas bag with laundry detergent and commanded me to wash its contents.

Every day I lived with anxiety, wondering how soon my only guardian would die from bleeding. Since I had to wash the rags late evening in the bathroom, I assumed that Florence didn't want anyone to know about the bleeding. I thought that it was a secret she wanted me to keep.

As I walked through a neighbor's yard one day, I noticed a small light-blue cardboard box with the word "Kotex" on it in a garbage can. I walked toward the box and stopped. In my mind, I was about to steal something. I wanted the box to make a toy car, with Coke bottle caps for wheels and buttons for headlights. While no one was watching, I took the box quickly, put it under my shirt, and fled. I hid it behind a bush at the side of Florence's house, waiting for free time to make a toy. After midday dinner, Florence lay down on her bed for her afternoon nap and called me in to scratch the bottom of her feet. I once heard that this was an activity female slaves used to perform for their mistresses. I despised this routine because I had to kneel at the foot of the bed on the mosaic floor, causing my abscessed right knee to hurt and ooze a foul-smelling liquid. Whenever I fell asleep at her feet, she would kick me in the face and shout, "You're going to scratch my feet until I fall asleep if I have to kick your head off, you extrait caca [essence of shit], you son of a whore." As Florence slept, I quietly left the room, thinking of the Kotex box I had hidden away. Once outside I crouched down and pulled the treasured box from the bush. I noticed several rolls of cloth material inside. I unrolled the first one and discovered a big blood stain on it. Confused, I dropped it and went back to the neighbor's yard. I watched everyone's exposed skin surreptitiously, hoping to discover the source of the blood. I returned home and disposed of the box.

I sat under the mango tree in the yard with my catechism trying to memorize as much as I could in preparation for my First Communion. As I recited passages, I visualized myself wearing long white pants, a white long-sleeved shirt, red bow tie, and shiny black shoes. Entering the church with my classmates, I was at the head of the line, holding a shiny black rosary. Standing behind the Communion rail, the priest said, "The body of Christ," and I answered, "Amen," as I opened my mouth to receive the Host. I didn't imagine a big dinner reception with a house full of friends and relatives who brought gifts and money for me, but I was certain that I was going to have my First Communion because my school—Ecole du Canada—was preparing a group of students for the sacrament. I was probably eight to ten years old at this time.

During classes on Saturday afternoons, everyone was eager to answer questions and display his knowledge of the Bible and catechism. Every class started the same way.

Teacher: What is a catechism?
Students: A catechism is a little book from which we learn the
          Catholic religion.
Teacher: Where is God?
Students: God is in heaven, on earth, and everywhere.

Teacher: Recite the Ten Commandments of God.
Students: Thou shalt not have other gods besides me.
          Thou shalt not . . .
          Thou shalt not . . .

Everyone responded to every question and command in unison and with enthusiasm. At the end of class, we told each other with gleaming eyes what our parents planned to prepare for dinner the day of Communion. It seemed that everyone's parents had been fattening either a goat or a turkey. Some talked about their trip to the tailor or the shoemaker. Everyone had a story to tell—even I, but my stories were all made up. During every trip back home, I thought about the First Commandment and wondered why Florence worshipped several other gods immediately after she returned home from church. She must have known about the Ten Commandments, because I read them in her prayer book every time she visited neighbors.

Saturday evening, the week before Confession, the students were very excited, knowing the day of their First Communion was getting closer. After class, everyone told stories of how his shoes and clothes were delivered or picked up. At home, I searched Florence's bedroom for new clothes and shoes and found nothing that belonged to me. I wanted to ask Florence if she had purchased the necessary clothes for me, but I could not, since I wasn't allowed to ask her questions. I considered asking her anyway and taking the risk of being slapped. But I couldn't vocalize the words—my fear of her was too intimidating. Thursday afternoon I searched again in every closet and under her bed and found nothing.

I began to worry. "Maybe she forgot," I thought. I placed the catechism on the dining room table as a reminder to Florence. She placed it on the kitchen table instead. "She remembers," I said to myself with a grin.

Friday afternoon, the eve of Confession, a street vendor was heard shouting her goods. "Bobby, call the vendor," yelled Florence. I ran to the sidewalk and summoned the woman vendor, who had coal-black skin and was balancing a huge yellow basket on top of her head. Several chickens of colorful plumage were hung upside down from her left forearm. Once in the yard and under the tree, she bent down and placed the pile of fowls on the ground. Florence's cook assisted her in freeing her head from the heavy load. After several minutes of bargaining, Florence bought two chickens. I felt very happy, thinking that a big dinner was being planned to celebrate my First Communion. But deep down inside, a small doubt lingered. Saturday morning, the eve of my First Communion, Florence left in a taxi. I had never been so happy. "Maman went to buy clothes for my First Communion," I told the cook, smiling, dancing, and singing. She paid no attention to me, but the expression on her face dampened my festive mood. By noon a taxi stopped in front of the house. I ran to see. It was Florence, carrying a big brown paper bag. I danced in my heart as I fought against the urge to hug her, knowing she would slap me away.

She walked in without saying a word. I went inside and fetched her slippers. She changed into another dress and began to supervise the cook who was preparing dinner. In the early afternoon, after I finished my chores, I approached Florence with a pail of water and a towel and began to wash her feet. She was sitting in her rocking chair, sipping sweet hot black coffee from a saucer. With pounding heart, I spoke. "Confession is at six o'clock and Communion is tomorrow at nine o'clock in the morning."

She stared at me for a long moment as she ground her teeth. Her faced turned very angry. "You little shithead bedwetter, you little faggot, you shoeshine boy. If you think I'm gonna spend my money on your First Communion, you're insane," she shouted. Trembling with fear, I dried her feet, slipped on her slippers, and stood up, holding the pail and towel. I felt as though my feet and legs were too heavy for me to move. I was stunned by her words. "Get out of my face," she yelled. I went into the kitchen and sat quietly in my usual corner without shedding a tear.

"Amelia!" called Florence loudly.

"Oui, Madame Cadet," the cook responded.

"You don't need to prepare the chicken for tomorrow; I'm spending the day with my niece. Her son is having his First Communion tomorrow," she said.

I went to her bedroom to find out the contents of the bag and saw a pair of shoes she intended to wear to her godson's First Communion. I felt crushed, but at the same time resigned myself to believe that only children with real mothers and fathers go to First Communion, receive presents from Santa Claus, and celebrate their birthdays.

2 **Every Saturday morning** Florence sat in her rocking chair under the huge tree in the front yard, waiting for her regular goat meat and pork vendors. Most of the time she purchased on credit and promised to pay the following week. "You know me, when it comes to paying my debts I am blanc," she would say in Creole to the vendors, who always replied, "Oui, Madame, I trust you." *Blanc* was a magic word that seemed to hypnotize vendors and creditors into submission. While Florence despised light-skinned women, she wished that she were a "mulâtresse." She washed her face three times a day with ice water, thinking that it would slow down the aging process and lighten her complexion. Occasionally she would rub her face with an ice cube as if she were trying to erase her blackness. Sometimes during a beating she would say to me, "Don't think you're better than I am because your skin is lighter than mine." She always said that a poor light-skinned woman was the equivalent of a rich, dark-skinned woman, and a rich light-skinned woman was above everyone else. Florence also believed that light-skinned women in Port-au-Prince were more sought after. As mistresses they were handsomely rewarded, and as wives they seemed to have the richest husbands.

Florence worshipped Maîtresse Erzulie, a fair-complexioned voodoo spirit, or loa, that resembled the Virgin Marie. She believed that Erzulie would bring her great wealth. Florence also believed in other loas called Ayida Ouedo, Damballa, and Saint Jacques Majeur. She enshrined the loas' pictures in the center of a custom-made mahogany cabinet. Every morning after she returned home from church, she lit cotton wicks in white porcelain bowls, placed them in front of the shrine, and sang voodoo songs until she seemed possessed. Once a week she sent me to buy roses and sometimes a bottle of rum to place in front of her treasured shrine.

The only advantage I had over other restavecs was that Florence allowed me to attend public school after my chores were done. At school, teachers referred to me as Jean-Robert Cadet, and at home Florence called me Bob or Bobby. While poor parents made financial sacrifices to purchase the necessary school materials for their children, Florence always told me to borrow books from other children and copy the pages into a notebook. Some days I didn't go to school at all because two of Florence's girlfriends would come to borrow me to clean their houses. Instead of thanking me for my services, they always said, "Tell Madame Cadet I said thank you." I preferred being at school to being borrowed, but preferred being borrowed to being at home, where I was routinely punched in the gut, slapped in the face, tugged by the ears, and pinched in the groin by Florence. I had one pair of tennis shoes, two khaki shorts, two shirts, and no underwear. At five-thirty in the morning, I picked up my bedding from the kitchen floor, filled the bathtub, collected Florence's chamber pot, set the table, and made a trip to the bakery. During Florence's breakfast, I cleaned the chamber pot, watered the plants, and swept the yard.

After breakfast I cleared the table and ate whatever was left while sitting on a small step stool in a corner of the kitchen. I washed the dishes before going to Ecole du Canada, which was two blocks away. Every morning the students stood in front of the flagpole at the entrance. Their tin cups, brought to receive free powdered milk, dangled from the pieces of ropes that held up their khaki shorts. While two students slowly hoisted the large white flag with the red maple leaf in the center, everyone pledged allegiance to Canada with their right hands over their hearts. "Oh Canada, terre de nos aieux [land of our forefathers] . . ." Every afternoon the flag was lowered with the same ceremony.

On rare occasions, when white visitors entered the classrooms, everyone rose and remained standing with gleaming eyes. The students' facial expressions seemed to indicate that these *blancs* who always distributed holy cards before they left were not from this earth. I looked at them with admiration, thinking that they were godlike. "I wonder if they use the bathroom like regular people," I asked myself. Florence's voice echoed in my mind: "When it comes to paying my debts, I am blanc." She sometimes said of her son, "When it comes to intelligence, my son is blanc."

During recess, the students would trade their cards. Those who by chance received pictures of black saints would leave their cards in the yard, because they believed that black saints did not answer prayers. Once I received two cards, one of the Virgin Marie and the other of Saint Joseph. After I gave my Saint Joseph to a classmate who had thrown away his black saint, we played Toussaint Louverture and Jean-Jacques Dessalines against the blancs, the same way American children played Cowboys and Indians. In a sense, we were reenacting the Haitian revolution that freed the slaves and created the first independent black republic in the Western Hemisphere. Every night I slept with the Virgin Marie card under my pillow, made of an old, folded-up dress.

The morning session started at nine o'clock and ended at noon, with a thirty-minute recess starting at ten o'clock. During that time I copied the assigned pages from other students' books. Going back home from school was always a frightening, heart-pounding experience for me. I always felt like a condemned man walking toward an electric chair. I recalled every detail of the morning, searching for mistakes I might have made, and prayed to God that I would find Florence in a good mood and that she had forgotten to inspect my bedding for wetness.

Before returning for the afternoon session at two o'clock, I dusted the furniture, set the table, washed Florence's feet, and filled the water bottles in the refrigerator. I liked the afternoon session the most because math was my favorite subject. At school, my comrades looked up to me, despite my restavec appearance. They assumed that I was intelligent because I had light skin. There were students of all ages in my class. We never discussed how old we were—it didn't seem important. In fact, I didn't know my age because Florence never told me.

Teachers gave me extra attention in class, sending me to the board more often than my peers. I was always selected to perform in small plays and given poems to memorize. When I was in about the third grade and Mother's Day was two weeks away, a group of students was being prepared to perform on stage for the occasion. I was selected to sing a solo called "Mother's Heart, I Sing for You That I Love." Early each afternoon, the participants eagerly filled a large room for rehearsal.

The choir was to dress in khaki shorts and white shirts. In addition, everyone was to wear a red carnation on his shirt. Those whose mothers were deceased would wear white carnations. I had the khaki shorts but not the white shirt. I knew the song so well that I could sing it in my sleep.

The morning of Mother's Day, Florence went to church and returned with a red carnation on her blouse. I was anxious to know if she had purchased the required white shirt. I waited until three o'clock, one hour prior to the performance. Then I approached Florence, trying to convey my anxiety without words. As she often did, Florence seemed to read my mind.

"Mérité pas mandé," she said in Creole, meaning, "Those who deserve don't ask." I dropped my head and walked away, thinking that I didn't deserve the shirt because I was a bedwetter. That afternoon, a car came to pick up Florence. She locked the house and left me in the yard until nightfall.

When teachers began to discover that I would never show up for the actual performance, they stopped choosing me for parts. Eventually they came to realize that I was a restavec who was allowed only to attend school.

Cooks also seemed to like me. Sometimes they covered for my mistakes or took the blame for chores that I had failed to perform. One particular cook, Matilda, was very fond of me. She would submerge my urine-soaked bedding in a large pail of water before Florence had a chance to inspect it. "Madame, the little boy didn't wet his bed; I'm washing his bedding for him," she would say.

Sometimes after a severe beating, Matilda would ask me, "Why don't you run away and go back to your family? I'll give you the bus fare and pack some food for you."

I was always confused by her suggestions because I couldn't remember ever having any other parents or being anywhere else.

"Did she ever tell you who your mother and father were?" asked the cook.

I repeated what Florence often told me during a beating: "Your mother was a dog and a whore, that's why your father doesn't want you. You're an embarrassment to him."

Matilda shook her head and said, "Jesus Marie Joseph." She could not save me from every beating because her chances were few and Florence's desire to inflict pain was unrelenting. Besides, she only worked from eight to five and could be fired at any time.

Every night at ten o'clock, I collected the chamber pot from the bathroom and placed it beside Florence's bed. Whenever she detected the smell of urine, she would put the pot over my head and shake it as if she were ringing a bell. The chamber pot had to be rewashed with mint leaves from her garden and returned to her bedroom. And I would sit in a corner of the kitchen, waiting for her to go to bed before spreading my rags on the cool mosaic floor. I would lie down, cover my body with an old dress, and listen to the monotonous hum of the refrigerator until I fell asleep. I would wake up early in the morning with palpitating heart in a pool of urine.

On occasion, restavecs managed to form friendships with other restavecs and play together when their "masters" were out for extended hours. I had met René, a boy about fourteen years old with a dark-brown complexion. He seemed a few years older than I was. I must have been between ten and twelve years old. René had been acquired by the Beauchamp family, who lived three houses away. Madame Beauchamp needed a permanent sitter for her two boys, and Monsieur Beauchamp, a tall and stingy mulatto, wanted someone to wash his small fleet of taxis every morning. René was thin, with a face that always looked hungry. He once told me that he had been acquired from a small village in Jérémi, and that his mother Dieudonne had named him Prophet. Every morning he woke up at the crowing of the first rooster to wash the cars before the drivers arrived. At eight o'clock in the evening he collected the car keys and the moneybags from the drivers. Between eight and nine o'clock at night, I would listen for René's signal—three long whistles. If I whistled back, we would meet behind Florence's house to watch *I Love Lucy* through the window screen, standing on cement blocks in the dark while mosquitoes feasted on our exposed arms and legs. When Florence had left the house and I was locked out at night, René and I would meet beside the Beauchamps' house to eat sugarcane under the almond tree and count passing cars. In the Beauchamps' living room, the television was placed under the window and restavecs were not allowed to watch it indoors. We rarely saw each other during daytime hours. René was always busy watching the children, and I had to be constantly within the reach of Florence's voice.

One beautiful moonlit night, the air was cool, the crickets were quarreling back and forth, and the mosquitoes were barely noticeable. The adventures of *Tarzan* had just started when René arrived nervously with a hand basket.

"What's in there?" I asked.

René pulled out a bowl of *grillot* (fried pork) and plantains, two bottles of Cola Couronne, and fresh pastries. We sat on the cement block and ate in silence with our fingers from the same bowl. I wanted to ask him where he got the money to buy the food, but I didn't want to know the answer. At the end of the show, René walked away without saying good-bye. I watched him disappear into the darkness as my heart beat faster than usual.

By midmorning, news had quickly spread among the maids and restavecs that René had stolen two dollars from Monsieur Beauchamp's cashbox. René was severely beaten with a *rigoise*—a whip made of cowhide. Every strike lifted the skin and formed a blister.

Monsieur Beauchamp wanted to know whether René had shared the money with other restavecs, but René did not implicate me. He was made to kneel on a bed of hot rocks, used by the maids to whiten clothes under the punishing tropical sun, while holding two mango-sized stones in each hand high above his head. After René blacked out, Monsieur Beauchamp threw him in the backseat of his car and drove to the police station.

The police brought René back late in the afternoon. His nose was bleeding, his eyes were swollen shut, and his lips resembled two pieces of raw cow's liver. His puffy face was twisted to one side and his ragged shirt was glued to his broken body. That night I listened for René's whistles that I knew would never be heard again. Although I never saw René again, I listened every night between eight and nine o'clock for the signal that I could hear only with my imagination.

The disappearance of René caused me to live in fear. I had always jumped and trembled at the angry sound of Florence's voice, but now the fear caused me to have diarrhea. Before he left, I used to wet my bed of old rags three to four times a week, for which I was beaten with either a broom handle or a martinet, a whip with leather strips and a wooden handle. Now the bed-wetting became a nightly occurrence and the beatings a daily routine. With each blow Florence said, grinding her teeth, "My son never wet his bed. Ever since I took you in, you've been wetting your bed. That's why you'll never have a mattress." On days when she was too busy to beat me, she waited for nighttime when I was asleep. After the first blow awakened me, I would tuck my chin against my chest, roll my body into a ball, and raise my shoulders to protect my face. Sometimes she didn't stop until the broom handle splintered.

3 **I was ill.** As usual, I didn't tell Florence. She had to discover my condition for herself, or the cook would say, "Madame Cadet, Bobby has a fever." Florence was always angry during times when I was sick because my chores would be left unattended. She had to empty her own chamber pot, wash it, and return it to her bedroom. A shoeshine boy, carrying a small wooden box and making musical tunes by ringing a small bell, was called in to shine her shoes. She kept me out of sight, allowing me to rest in a corner of her room on the pile of rags that served as my bedding until I recuperated. I became the responsibility of the cook.

This arrangement was good for me because I was able to communicate my needs. The cook nursed me back to health with three different kind of teas: vervain with brown sugar in the morning, garlic skin with rock salt at noon, and a bitter vine with rock salt in the evening that made me grimace, gave me goose bumps, and caused saliva to drip from my lower lip. After serving me a break-

fast of tomato soup with bread, she boiled orange, lemon, and guanabana leaves in a large pot and let it sit in the sun. Then she took
me outside and poured my own warm urine over my head before
bathing me with the boiled leaves. Afterward, she helped me back
to my bedding and covered me with two of Florence's old dresses.

To elevate my head, she placed a small wooden chair face down
on the floor, using the back of it as my pillow. On Florence's bed
were two pillows in beautifully embroidered cases, but the cook
would not dare to place one under my head because she knew that
I was a restavec, not a blood relative of Florence's. Knowing that I
was a bedwetter, she woke me up three to four times a day from
my sleep to make me use the bathroom. If my bedding was wet, I
would have to sit in a chair until the rags had dried in the sun. Although there was a medical clinic a block away from the house,
Florence would not take me in for a doctor's visit. It was socially
unacceptable for the member of an affluent family to be seen waiting in a free clinic with a restavec.

Florence never used home medicine or urine to cure her son,
Denis, when he was sick. Medical doctors visited him and wrote
prescriptions.

While I was sick, I was wakened late one night. My bedding
was wet. The room was dark and Florence's bed was shaking. I was
frightened by the moaning of Florence and that of a man. I stood
by the bed and said, "You're hurting Maman! You're hurting Maman!" Suddenly I heard Florence's voice shouting, "Shut up and
get out!" I ran to the door, groping for the doorknob. I went to the
dark kitchen and squatted in the corner, sobbing uncontrollably.

After a while, Florence came out and pulled the light cord. I
lifted my head and made eye contact with her. She opened the
door and the man, who appeared familiar to me, exited the house.
"Go back to sleep," she ordered with a harsh tone. I followed Florence to her room and separated the wet rags from the dry ones.
She dumped a basketful of dirty laundry in front of me and said,
"Sleep on these." After I fixed my bedding, she turned out the
light. Not a word was uttered. As I laid my head on the back of the
chair that served as my pillow, I wondered why Maman had allowed that man to hurt her. When I recovered from my sickness, I

returned to my routine of sleeping on the kitchen floor and received the usual treatment. But every time I looked at Florence, I
thought about the night when I saw her in bed with that man. I
wondered again and again why she had allowed him to hurt her.

The man returned, usually on Saturday nights. His black car
was always parked in the street in front of the house. After a few
moments in the living room, he would follow Florence into her
room. Different men were coming to visit her almost every night.
To these men—called Roland, Albert, Roger, and several other
names—I was as significant as a family pet. I was convinced that
the men were responsible for Florence's bleeding and wished that I
could stop them from coming to the house. I visualized myself
shooting them like cowboys shot Indians in the movies. Since no
guns were available in the house, I did the next best thing—I let
the air out of their tires.

4   **One hot Saturday noon,** a taxi dropped off Florence and her best friend, Claudette Estimé, who
frequently borrowed me. She was a beautiful dark-
skinned Negress in her early thirties who reminded me of a giant
Coca-Cola bottle. Sometimes when I followed her home, I watched
her swing her big hips from side to side to slow up traffic. Whenever she was given a ride home, I was always left behind to continue on foot. Like Florence, she was the mistress of several influential men. The two women sat in the shade of the mango tree in
the backyard.

"Bobby," called Florence. Within seconds, I appeared in front of
her, barefoot, arms hanging at my sides, staring straight-faced.

"Bring Mademoiselle Claudette and me some ice water."

I replied with a simple "Oui," and made an about-face to carry
out her orders. As I reached for the glasses on the top shelf of
the cabinet, a glass fell down and shattered. Suddenly my heart
raced and I began to shake. I broke into a cold sweat. My stomach
grumbled.

"What did you break, you son of a bitch?" yelled Florence. I
placed two glasses and a bottle of ice water on a tray and went out-

side to serve the two women. Florence looked at me with fire in her eyes and repeated the question: "What did you break?"

"A-a-a gla-glass, " I stuttered, sobbing.

"I don't want to be upset right now. I'll take care of you later," she said calmly. I placed the tray on a small iron table next to Mademoiselle Claudette. As I began to pour the water, Claudette reached out and took the bottle from my trembling hand. "Go kneel by the door," Florence said, pointing at the entrance to the kitchen.

I followed her instruction and placed my bare knees on the cement step and crossed my arms against my chest. As the two women talked and laughed in the background, I had a vision of René's face and wondered whether or not Florence was going to take me to the police station for a beating. My thoughts were suddenly interrupted by the cooing of pigeons on the edge of the rooftop. As I gazed at them, I wished that I could somehow turn myself into a pigeon and fly away.

A loud "Come here!" from Florence startled me. Mademoiselle Claudette had just left.

I rose slowly to my feet, for the muscles behind my legs had tightened. Florence was impatient, moving back and forth in her rocking chair. I walked slowly toward her, anticipating being held by the skin of my stomach and slapped several times across the face. I stood helplessly in front of her with quivering lips and watery eyes. She locked her jaw and ground her teeth. Florence reached between my legs and held me by the testicles with her thumb and index finger, preventing me from pulling away. As I was about to drop to my knees, she removed her shoe and struck me across the face. The spiked heel made a deep cut in the corner of my right eye, sending a very sharp pain through my head. I let out a scream. Florence stopped as she noticed blood oozing from the side of my face.

I ran toward the kitchen. Matilda quickly soaked her white canvas apron in cold water and held it over my eye, cleaning the mixture of blood and tears off my face while Florence disappeared into her bedroom to worship her loas. In disbelief, Matilda shook her head and said, "Jesus Marie Joseph."

My right eye swelled shut. For several days, I could only see with my left eye. That Saturday afternoon, Florence didn't call me in to scratch the bottom of her feet. I wished that she would die during her nap, knowing if she did die I wouldn't have anywhere to go. To my dismay, the word *maman* became very hard for me to say and soon disappeared from my vocabulary. Later that afternoon Matilda performed my chores and served me a plate of red bean soup over cornmeal with a piece of goat meat. After Florence woke from her nap, she stared at my face with a blank expression. She turned to Matilda and said, "Marinate the chicken for tomorrow before you go."

"Oui, Madame," she answered sharply. Matilda boiled a pot of water and gathered old newspapers with which to pluck and flambé the bird after she killed it. She untied the chicken, plucked under its neck, and ran the blade across its throat. As blood dripped from the knife, she threw down the bird to thrash about before it died. Instead, it landed on its feet. When Matilda reached down to grab it, it ran out of the yard. She called me for help. With my right eye swollen shut, I combed the neighborhood, asking people if they had seen a chicken with a bloody neck running by. Some people said "Non" and laughed, while others boldly said, "If I find it, I will eat it." After a while, we returned empty-handed to an angry Florence, who promptly fired Matilda and deducted the price of the chicken from her pay.

In the early evening, after I washed Florence's feet, she sent me to Claudette's house to do housework. I washed dishes, cleaned the bathroom, and dusted her bedroom. Claudette had prepared a variety of dishes: goat meat, chicken, red beans and rice, yams, corn pudding, popcorn, and roasted peanuts. These were dished into small calabash bowls of different shapes and sizes and meticulously arranged on a large mat in a corner of the living room. Flickering candlelight, reflected against the shine of the multicolored mosaic floor, made the room mysteriously somber. Pale gray smoke from incense sticks snaked lazily toward the ceiling. The smell of tafia, a strong liquor made from sugarcane, seemed to stand guard at the entrance. Against a wall stood an open double-door mahogany cabinet. Inside it was decorated with colorful supernatural pictures of white people. The most visible portrait resembled a well-dressed Roman soldier on horseback fighting a multiheaded serpent with a sword.

Claudette's few guests—mostly dark-skinned black men—sat in chairs along the wall, wiping their sweaty brows with red handkerchiefs. In the center of the room was Claudette, singing a song about Saint Jacques Majeur and dancing like a puppet on strings. She then walked around the room, greeting each guest with a firm handshake. She picked up a bottle of rum from the mat and poured several drops in each corner of the room while mumbling the names of her loas.

After her ritual, she glanced casually at my injured eye and instructed me to clean the floor. She placed a few bowls of food in a brown paper bag. "On your way home, place these bowls in the middle of the intersection where the road is unpaved," she said. I walked outside with the bag. The cloudless sky and the deserted streets were lit by a full and overly bright moon. I ran a little and walked a little until I reached the chosen crossroads. In the distance, the rhythmic tam-tam of a lone drum traveled through the silence of the night. I was frightened. My heart pounded against my chest as I removed the three bowls one by one from the bag. After placing them in the middle of the road, I ran to Florence's house, thinking of my last chore: placing the chamber pot under her bed.

5 **Florence's son, Denis,** moved in. The men stopped coming to visit. Denis was about to marry a tall, light-skinned woman named Lise. Lise's mother came to visit. She was a dark-skinned voodoo priestess whom Florence referred to as a mambo. Judging from her daughter and her two sons' complexions, her husband must have had light skin. Florence told friends that Lise's mother was not too thrilled about the union because Denis's skin was too dark and his profession—administrator in a public works project—lacked prestige.

The day of the wedding, I spent the whole morning cleaning the house and sweeping the yard. By early afternoon, people were bringing the bride's furniture and clothes. A Coca-Cola truck with a huge picture of Tonton Noël (Santa Claus) on the back pulled in and delivered several cases of Cokes. The wedding cakes were placed in the living room. I was curious. I wondered out aloud, "What's going on?"

Well-dressed guests of all ages were arriving and waiting in the living room.

"Bobby, bring a mop," said Florence. A child had spilled his drink. As I walked into the living room, holding the mop, I stared at the dark-skinned boy about my age and, for a few seconds, our eyes met. I was admiring his white shirt, blue suit, and shiny black shoes. The expression on the boy's face seemed to indicate that my odor had just offended his nose. I felt uncomfortable and out of place. My shirt was dirty and the buttons were missing. My filthy khaki shorts had a split from the crotch to the belt loop and my buttocks were exposed.

I made three trips to the living room to clean up spills, and each time I walked out backward, staring at the floor, making sure that no one caught sight of my derriere. Then I took my place in the corner of the kitchen, waiting for the next call.

The bride and groom walked in. I lifted my head and realized for the first time that the guests were here to celebrate a wedding.

After everyone left, Florence secured the rest of the cake and hors d'oeuvres. I returned to the living room at Florence's command and cleared the paper plates off the table. I grabbed unfinished bites of cake and furtively tossed them into my mouth as fast as I could. After I finished my chores, I sat on the small footstool in the corner of the kitchen, waiting for Florence's signal to spread out my bedding and go to sleep.

When the couple returned from their honeymoon, they brought back a young girl about thirteen years old. Her skin, which was a shade lighter than coal, seemed like it had been rubbed with a dirty blackboard eraser. Judging from her appearance, I knew immediately that she was a restavec. Her luggage consisted of a cardboard box with the word "Carnation" printed in red and a rolled-up mat secured tightly with a piece of rope.

Her hair was done in four short braids, one on each side, one on top, and one in the back. The reflection of the sun was visible on the part in her hair. Her eyes were big and somber, her ears pierced and naked. Her nose was broad and flat; her face oval and anorexic. Her expression was robotic and she seemed incapable of smiling. Her collarbones showed beneath her pink patterned dress and her chest was flat. Her knees were rough and dry, her dusty feet visibly resting inside dirty plastic sandals.

She gave me a look that said "Stay away from me." I resented her. We gave each other dirty looks every time our eyes met. The tension grew as the hours passed.

Lise guided her to the bathroom and showed her where to put her box. She changed into her work clothes and Lise handed her a pile of lingerie to wash. She had been Lise's restavec and now she came to continue her old chores. She was not introduced to either me or the cook. Her instructions came only from Lise.

She prepared Lise's bath and assisted her in the bathroom. She, like myself, spoke only when spoken to. I learned her name when she was called to perform a chore.

"Anita," called Lise.

"Plaît-il [if it pleases you], Madame," she answered quickly. As she scrubbed the laundry next to the rock pile, I went into the bathroom and searched her cardboard box. She had two dresses, a nightgown, two or three pairs of underwear, a black oily comb with a few missing teeth, and a small bottle of dark-brown oil for her hair.

Lise came out with a paper bag and handed it to Anita. It contained Lise's old toothbrush, a used bar of soap, and some old clothes that were too big for Anita. "Merci, oui," she said, taking the bag.

As I observed, I became jealous of Anita because she had underwear and I didn't. As soon as Lise was out of sight, I pinched her in the back of the neck and ran. As I returned to pinch her again, she grabbed a rock and said angrily, "Little boy, leave me alone or I'll split your head open." I looked in her eyes and backed off.

Anita helped in the kitchen and set the table for dinner. After the adults ate, the cook dished out the cornmeal prepared especially for restavecs. It was cooked in salted water and a teaspoon of lard. She gave Anita and me each a plateful with leftover sauce from the table. I sat on the small footstool in one corner of the kitchen while Anita squatted in the other. I ate with a spoon while she ate with her fingers, and we drank water from our respective tin cups.

As we traded dirty looks like boxers trading punches, Denis stood at the entrance eating a piece of leftover wedding cake. Staring at the two of us, he began tossing specks of hard frosting at our plates. Sometimes he missed, but when he hit the plate he grinned delightedly. Anita and I ate the frosting out of fear of what might happen if we didn't.

After dinner, I performed my usual chores of washing the car and shining everyone's shoes. Anita did the dishes and continued with Lise's laundry.

I was more afraid of Denis than Florence. When Denis was near, my heart seemed to beat a lot faster.

On Sunday afternoons, Lise prepared special desserts for Denis. When she made ice cream, it was always my job to turn the handle of the ice cream churn, sitting on the small step stool facing the three adults who sat comfortably in their rocking chairs under the mango tree that dominated the backyard like a giant umbrella and switching hands as my arms got tired. On one occasion, Denis leaned over to one side and passed gas loudly. As he chuckled, he knocked me off the stool with his foot. "You little pig, can't you say 'Excuse me'?" he said. Florence and Lise laughed loudly. Without raising my head to make eye contact, I nervously said "Pardon" and continued turning the handle. A precedent was set. Every time an adult passed gas, I was compelled to say "Excuse me."

When the ice cream was ready, Lise served her husband, her mother-in-law, herself, and then placed the rest in the freezer. Not a drop was given to either Anita or me. Not cake or ice cream or any other kind of dessert was wasted on restavecs—nor, for that matter, any meaty part of a chicken or a turkey. I tasted the ice cream nonetheless: I licked the bowls before washing them.

When nightfall approached, husband, wife, and mother-in-law installed themselves in the living room to watch television. I ran to the back of the house and stood on a cement block to watch *I Love Lucy* through the open curtains. Although the episodes were in English, I managed to laugh.

"Anita!" called Lise. I startled.

"Plaît-il, Madame," she answered, running to Lise.

"You can go to the back to watch television with Bobby," she instructed. "Oh no, I am not gonna share my block with a girl," I thought.

Anita came near me and tried to share my block. I pushed her down. "Go find your own cement block," I whispered to her. Suddenly I remembered my friend René. I was determined not to share my block with a girl I didn't like. Anita returned to the kitchen and sat in the corner staring at the blank wall, waiting to be told when and where to make her bedding.

At eleven o'clock, the television was turned off. I performed my last chores and made my bed on the kitchen floor as usual. Anita was told to sleep in the dining room. She made her bed under the table, changed into her long nightgown, and lay down in a fetal position. An old dress folded into a ball served as her pillow.

In the morning, as she was gathering her bedding, I noticed a large wet spot on her mat. After spreading her mat on the rock pile to dry, she mopped the floor.

It seemed that all the restavecs I knew wet their bedding. I would see the wet brown mats drying in the morning sun over rock piles, fences, and small bushes when I ran errands.

After a few days, I warmed up to Anita. When the adults left for extended evening hours, they locked the doors and gave each of us a penny to buy our supper. We each purchased five small mangoes from a street corner vendor sitting under a streetlamp. We would eat the mangoes in the dark to avoid seeing fruitworms.

Every time we found ourselves all alone in the yard, Anita's face seemed less mechanical and the somber expression would disappear from her eyes. Although she could neither read nor write her own name, she was a good storyteller. She once told me the story of a married couple. The husband suspected his wife of being a loup-garou, or a werewolf. On certain nights, when the moon was full, the wife—who really was a loup-garou—would remove her skin, hide it under the bed, and fly out to search for victims whose blood she would suck. She always returned before sunrise. One particular night the husband, who pretended to be asleep, sprinkled salt and pepper onto the skin as soon as his wife flew out of the house. When she returned, the skin stung her each time she tried to put it back on. As soon as the sun rose, the husband jumped out of bed and opened all the windows. Unable to tolerate sunlight, the loup-garou screamed as she shriveled up and died.

"Cric?" said Anita, smiling like a sick child.

"Crac," I eagerly answered.

"You go this way, I'll go the other way, and we'll meet," she continued, with music in her voice.

"A belt," I responded, having heard the riddle at least a thousand times.

"Cric?" she said immediately.

"Crac," I responded again.

"A ball in a hole," she said.

"Your head in a hat," I replied.

We continued with the game until we were interrupted by two bright headlights and the familiar sound of Denis's car.

I found Anita a tree stump on which to stand when the television was turned on in the living room. Her health was fragile. She caught fever often and always depended on the generosity of the cook for home medicine.

Lise made sure that Anita worked in the kitchen as often as possible so she could eventually replace the cook.

One early Saturday afternoon, Lise decided to put Anita to the test. She ordered the frail child to kill and marinate a chicken for Sunday's dinner. Knowing that her every move was being watched, Anita seemed overpowered by fear. The mannerisms that made her the little girl that she was had vanished. Anita shook like a palsied old woman as she placed a pot of water on the coal stove. Armed with a knife, she clumsily grabbed the uncooperative bird and cut the thin rope from its leg. As the terrified animal struggled to be free, Anita dropped her weapon and subdued her opponent by kneeling on its wings. Holding its neck back in her left hand, she recovered the knife and severed its head after several strokes. Blood squirted from its veins and stained her blouse. As the dying bird thrashed violently on the ground, Anita rose to her bare feet trembling with the bloody knife in her hand. There was silence.

Anita carried the lifeless bird to the kitchen and plunged it into the boiling water to loosen its feathers. She plucked the bird, held it over flaming newspapers, and dissected it to Lise's specifications. After the chicken was marinated, she placed it in the refrigerator for Sunday's dinner.

Lise handed Anita a few drops of olive oil in a cup. "Clean the guts and eat them for your supper," she said. I, who was within hearing distance but out of Lise's sight, could not believe my ears. I had never heard of anyone cooking and eating chicken guts before.

"Oui, Madame," answered Anita.

"Use an old pot or a tin cup. Don't use the regular pots," added Lise.

"Oui, Madame," answered Anita. She turned the guts inside out, then washed and sautéed them in the oil while I watched in disbelief.

"You want some?" asked Anita, offering me a piece of curled-up chicken gut.

I made a face. "Non, merci," I said. Anita ate the guts like something she was accustomed to eating.

At that moment, my dislike for Lise became obvious, something she discovered for herself when she made eye contact with me. And I soon found anger in Denis's face whenever I made eye contact with him. Denis's eyes seemed to say, I don't like you if you don't like my wife. He would kick and shove me aside whenever our paths crossed.

Lise seemed to get pleasure out of watching me being beaten by either her husband or her mother-in-law, because these were the only times she gave me those sinister smiles that seemed to say "That's the price you pay for giving me dirty looks." She watched my every move, making sure that I escaped no punishment. Sometimes she would close the curtains on my face while I watched television from the outside of the house.

Early one Saturday evening, I was stealing ice cream from the refrigerator. As I was about to put the spoon in my mouth, I felt a presence behind me. My heart raced. I turned my head. It was Lise. "Enjoying my ice cream?" she asked with cold eyes and a fake smile.

I stood before her trembling with fear. She walked away and went outside to join Florence. I held the spoon, full of ice cream, unable to decide what to do with it.

"Bobby," yelled Florence. I quickly opened the freezer and put back the ice cream.

"Plaît-il," I answered, running out before she called my name a second time.

I stood before Florence, still shaken. "Go put on your shoes. I want to send you to the store," she said. I breathed a sigh of relief.

"She didn't tell," I said to myself. I looked at Lise and she gave me that same sinister smile. I walked away, thinking "I am free." I went to the bathroom to put on my shoes. I opened my cardboard box. One shoe was missing. Searching frantically, I began to shake.

"Did you remove one of my shoes?" I asked Anita.

"Non," she answered.

"I am dead, she's going to kill me." I told her. Anita helped me look everywhere in the bathroom.

Florence yelled for me again and I quickly put on the one shoe and ran outside. I stood before Florence, hiding the naked foot behind the shoed foot. Lise lowered the *Paris-Match* from her face.

"Where is your other shoe?" she asked.

Before I could answer, Florence looked at my feet and asked, "Where is the other shoe?" with anger in her eyes.

"I can't find it," I answered.

She sent me back to find the other shoe, and I searched everywhere to no avail.

"Bobby," yelled Florence. I rushed outside again and stood in front of Florence.

"I can't find the other shoe," I told her. Lise's eyes remained fixed in her magazine. Florence reached for my crotch and held me tightly. She removed her sandal and began to beat me on my head and face while Lise kept her eyes in her magazine. Florence stopped when it seemed that her arm was fatigued, and after that I ran errands and went to school barefoot.

A short time later, Anita became ill. She was coughing constantly. The cook was helping her get better, giving her a variety of salted tea and washing her head with boiled orange leaves and

Anita's warm urine. The clinic was only a block away, yet no one took her for a doctor's visit. One afternoon I returned home from school and discovered that Anita's cardboard box and bedroll were missing. I waited until morning and asked the cook what had happened to Anita.

"She was not getting better. Madame Denis sent her home to her mother," she replied. Anita was put in a taxi and I never saw her again.

I decided not to make eye contact with Lise anymore. Although she never physically punished me, I was more afraid of her than of Denis and Florence.

Early one Saturday afternoon, I was sitting on the rear bumper of the car, playing with matches and a piece of candle that Florence had thrown out from her voodoo cabinet. "Are you trying to burn my car?" yelled Denis angrily.

"Non," I replied as fear caused my stomach to turn. Denis knocked me down with a slap across the face. He returned inside and came back out with an extension cord. After the first strike, I urinated on myself. The cord ripped my shirt and broke my skin. I was soon bloodied. I screamed as loudly as I could, hoping Florence would intervene, but she didn't. Denis perspired so much that he had to shower before leaving.

I had so many blisters that I could not sit comfortably in a chair, and sleeping on my back was even more unbearable.

Denis only whipped me twice. The second time was when he caught me washing a neighbor's car. I wanted money to buy paper with which to make a kite. Denis was furious because his car had not yet been washed.

"How dare you wash someone else's car while my car is so muddy?" he said. He went inside to get the extension cord. Since he couldn't find it, he sent me to borrow a cowhide from a family who had two restavecs.

"You're going to get twenty lashes. Each time you raise your hands, I will start over again," he said. I stood erect with my arms pressed tightly to my sides. I clenched my teeth and closed my eyes. My face grimaced as I counted each blow as it landed on my back. After the last blow, I dropped to my knees. "Go kneel behind the chair," ordered Denis. I stood up. Not a tear fell. As I placed my knees on the lower cross-bar of the chair, I made eye contact with Florence and then lowered my head.

"Extrait caca, son of a bitch. Don't you know who feeds you? How can you wash somebody else's car instead of his? I am ashamed of you. I gave you my name and you don't respect it. I should have named you Bobby Joseph—anything but Bobby Cadet," said Florence. *Joseph* was a common name in Haiti, the equivalent of *Smith* or *Jones*.

After I knelt for a long time against the chair, Denis ordered me to shine the shoes and wash the car. "I don't want to see a speck of mud on it," he snapped. It was difficult to get up; my legs had fallen asleep.

I approached Denis, "Please forgive me. I will never wash the neighbor's car again," I said, staring at the ground. I went in to get the shoes. Under Florence's bed I discovered the extension cord Denis had been looking for. I wondered who could have hidden it under the bed. It was always on the table next to the electric mixer. I took the shoes outside along with a shoebox containing shoe polish, rags, and brushes. After I shined the shoes, I took them back inside. As I was placing Florence's shoes under her bed, I noticed that the extension cord was missing. Someone had placed it back on the table where it belonged. I suspected the cook was trying to save my skin.

6 **Lise was about** six months pregnant with her first child. I was kept out of school indefinitely. Making eye contact with Lise was no longer detrimental to me, and she had stopped watching my every move. Unlike her husband, who called me "you little pig," she always called me by my name. She had stopped closing the curtains in my face when I watched television from behind the house.

I always suspected that Lise had something to do with the disappearance of my shoe. I had kept the lone shoe in my box in case the other one turned up. It never did.

Florence and Lise did not like one another. They tolerated each other to please Denis. It was important to him that his wife and mother like each other.

I was so afraid of Denis that I made a conscious effort to stay out of his sight as much as possible. I shined his shoes when they did not need shining, prepared his bath every evening when he returned home from work, and cleaned his car inside and out every day. Denis had a solution for turning me into a more efficient worker and for correcting my bed-wetting problem or anything else he thought was wrong with me. Every time Florence belittled or beat me, Denis would say, "Let me take him to the police station. One good police beating will straighten him out for good." Each time he offered this suggestion, the image of a badly beaten René flashed into my mind. The occasion Denis had been waiting for finally presented itself. I was caught by the cook pouring water into the pot of milk to replace the amount I had stolen. The cook was furious. She did not want to take the blame for the diluted milk. I begged her not to tell, but she told Florence while the three were sitting in the yard drinking Coca-Cola. "Madame, Bobby has stolen some of the milk and he was trying to replace it with water," she said.

"Where is the little pig?" asked Denis.

"He's in the kitchen, crying," answered the cook.

"Get him out here," said Denis.

The cook went into the kitchen. "Monsieur Denis wants to see you," she said to me. My bowels moved. I rushed to the bathroom.

"Where is the little pig?" yelled Denis again. The cook ran out.

"He's in the bathroom," she announced. I went outside and appeared before the trio with my head down.

"Get in the car. I am taking you to the police station. That will teach you not to steal ever again," he said. I gazed into Florence's eyes, trying to say silently to her, "Please save me."

"Don't I feed you, you little thief?" shouted Florence angrily.

I walked toward the car, visualizing the bloody face of René. As I touched the rear door handle, Denis stood up. "I am gonna get my keys," he said as he went inside. I took off as fast as I could, running in the direction of my school, Ecole du Canada. Dusk had just settled. The school grounds were deserted. I walked frantically around the one-story building, pulling every window until I found one that was unlocked. I crawled into a classroom, locked the window, and hid under the teacher's desk. When I could not see light through the cracks of the shuttered windows, I climbed up on the desk and slept in a fetal position.

I was awakened early in the morning by the horns of cars and trucks. I spent that whole day in the school yard and in the classroom, practicing my long division and multiplication on the blackboard until hunger forced me to quit.

Before darkness fell, I went to a neighbor's yard and a maid gave me a plate of food, which I devoured with my hands while sitting on the dark porch on a small stool. I looked across the street to see if Denis's car was in the driveway. The yard seemed deserted. "I think Madame Denis went to the hospital to have the baby," said the neighbor's maid. As I walked home, I looked at the shutters. There was no light anywhere in the house. The night was dark and muggy, and the sky seemed bare. I stood under the mango tree and noticed that the rocking chairs had been moved inside. I leaned against the tree, reciting "Our Father which art in heaven," as I had practiced it in catechism class in preparation for my First Communion. Every time the lights of a car penetrated the thick darkness, my heart raced to my throat. Soon a car drove in. I stood frozen in the blinding light beams. The car stopped but the lights stayed on, the engine still humming. After a while, the engine turned silent and the light beams vanished. I was disoriented and petrified.

Denis and Florence stepped out of the car. The sound of his keys broke the silence.

"Bobby, you son of a bitch, get the bag out of the car," said Florence. Without a word, I rushed to the car and removed a large bag filled with foodstuffs from the backseat. I followed the two adults inside and placed the bag on the kitchen table while watching Denis and Florence from the corner of my eye.

"That's your dinner," said Florence, pointing to a plate of food on the coal stove. As I sat on the step stool to eat, Florence came out of her room. "When you're done, clean the chamber pots and put them in the bedrooms," she said calmly.

"Oui," I said, gazing at my plate of cornmeal covered with red bean sauce.

"It must be a trap. Maybe the police are on their way to get me," I said to myself.

After eating a portion of the food, I washed the chamber pots. I knocked on Denis's door.

"Come in," he said calmly. I felt disoriented by fear.

I slowly turned the doorknob and walked in. Denis was in bed. His eyes met mine. He said nothing but his face was full of anger. I placed the chamber pot beside his bed, walked out, and closed the door behind me. Then I knocked on Florence's door.

"Come in," she said. I walked in. She too was in bed but seemed relaxed. I placed the pot beside the bed, walked out, and closed the door behind me.

"Maybe they're waiting to beat me in my sleep," I said to myself. I looked at the clock in the living room. It was half past ten. I fixed my bedding in the usual place and lay down. I fought off sleep as long as I could, thinking that I was about to be whipped with the electrical cord. I was awakened early in the morning by the wetness of the rags under my back. The cook came to work.

"Little boy, where did you go?" she asked. I gave her a look that said, "Leave me alone and don't talk to me."

Before the week ended, Lise came home from the hospital with a little girl. I heard that her name was Emilie. Throughout the day people were coming to visit, bringing gifts for the newborn. I was curious about the baby. By midafternoon, I was yet to be invited into Lise's bedroom to see Emilie. I tried to stay out of sight as much as possible, hoping everyone would forget my running away.

"Bobby," yelled Florence. I startled. My heart seemed to have skipped a beat before it jumped to my throat. She handed me a brown paper bag. "Go take a bath and put these on," she said. "Merci, oui," I said without verifying its contents. I knew that it was new clothes, because she always waited until the ones on my back turned into rags before giving me new ones.

I took the bag to the bathroom and pulled out of it two pairs of khaki shorts and two shirts. After I bathed, I pulled out an old skirt from my box which had been given to me to use as my own towel. Denis had insisted that old bath towels in the house be used in the cleaning of his car to prevent scratch marks. I got dressed and appeared before Florence. "These clothes you're wearing are not yours. I am lending them to you. Every time you go near the baby, you will wear clean clothes," she said.

"Oui," I replied.

"You can go see the baby. Knock before you go in," she said.

I went back inside. Lise's bedroom door was ajar. Before I started to knock, Lise said, "Come in" as though she had been expecting me. I walked in hesitantly. Lise greeted me with a smile that seemed genuine. The dark-skinned newborn was sleeping peacefully beside her. "You've come to see Emilie. Come closer," she said. I leaned over the bed and smiled at the sleeping baby. Realizing that I didn't have a gift for her, I excused myself for a moment and returned with my prized possession, a toy car I had made from an empty box of soap powder and placed it next to Emilie. Lise smiled again. Motherhood had temporarily compelled her to see me as a human being. "Why don't you save it for her? She's too small to enjoy it right now," she said. I walked out with the toy and returned it to my cardboard box.

My new chores of boiling baby bottles, washing diapers, and feeding and baby-sitting Emilie kept me out of school. My relationship with Emilie was symbiotic. I was like a second mother to her, while she served as the protector of my skin. As long as I was near her, no physical harm would come to me.

Soon preparation for Emilie's baptism was underway. Lise wanted someone influential to be the godfather, her way of securing early social advantages for her daughter's future. Denis chose his mother as godmother. A turkey was prepared and several guests were invited. Emilie's presence changed the whole atmosphere in the house. She was everyone's priority. Lise insisted that proper French be spoken in Emilie's presence instead of Creole. She corrected my grammar every time I made an error and encouraged me to sing French songs to her little princess.

Lise threw a big dinner party. Coca-Cola was delivered ahead of time. Emilie's godfather, a tall, well-dressed mulatto, arrived with his camera. Another guest, a dark-skinned woman, handed me a small brown puppy. "This is for Emilie. Get him some milk, will you?" she ordered. I poured some of Emilie's leftover Similac formula from her baby bottles into a dish for the dog and saved some for myself. Denis, Lise, and Florence seemed to pay more attention to the mulatto than any other guest. He was always served first, and French was always spoken in his presence instead of Creole. He was the center of attention. When dinner was over, a large table was set in the backyard for ice cream, cake, and *crémasse*, a homemade coconut liqueur. Lise took Emilie from me. "Go eat and hurry back out," she said. The cook gave me a plate of leftover food and shared with me Coca-Cola that was left from a few opened bottles.

After I ate, I sat on a large mat away from the guests, feeding the baby. The puppy was beside me. The godfather approached the mat with his camera. As he was about to take a few pictures, Denis said, "Don't waste your film on him," taking his daughter from my arms and waving me away. After the mulatto took a few shots of Emilie in the arms of Denis with the dog in the background, Denis returned the baby to me and I resumed my motherly role.

7 **Christmas was coming.** The song "Petit Papa Noël" was heard from radios everywhere. The air was sweetened with the smell of homemade jams. Turkeys, waiting to be killed for Christmas and New Year's Eve, gobbled back and forth in the yards of the affluent. Women street vendors in colorful clothes balancing huge baskets on their heads seemed to shout their goods louder than usual.

I had stopped wishing for those cowboy boots I always wanted because every year Florence told me the same thing: "Tonton Noël never brings presents to bedwetters." But by the age of six I knew that Tonton Noël didn't like restavecs.

On Christmas morning, several gifts were waiting for Emilie in the living room. "How can she get all those presents? She wets her diapers constantly," I said to myself.

I blamed my bedwetting problem on my penis. I thought about

cutting it off to see if I would stop. I had taken a knife in hand several times, but I just could not find the courage to go through with it. I had tied it with a string one Christmas Eve, but severe stomach pain awakened me before sunup. Then I began to measure the amount of water I drank every day against the amount I passed. I had two identical tin cans. One was kept in the kitchen and the other was hidden in a bush beside the house. I drank from one and peed in the other. I thought that if I urinated the same amount I had drunk during the day, I wouldn't wet my bedding. I couldn't understand why my experiment never worked and was too ashamed to discuss it with the cook.

Every January first, poor children and familiar street vendors came to the yard asking for *étrenne*, a New Year's gift. They were usually given a few cents. On Christmas and New Year's Day, the cook and I were given rice and beans with leftover sauce from the table, instead of the usual cornmeal, and a bottle of cola to share.

Before sunset on that pleasant day of January first when Emilie was a baby, I put on my clean clothes and followed the cook to a large open field near Park Champ-de-Mars to watch the *masuiffé*, the climbing of a greasy telephone pole. At the very top of the pole, people said, "l'Etat," the police, placed one hundred gourdes (twenty dollars) and a sausage. Thousands of spectators gathered around the pole to witness this momentous event. Several climbers came with small shoulder bags, called *macoutes*, full of dirt to throw on the pole to reduce the slipperiness and create traction.

One man ran to the pole and climbed as fast as he could, while another followed suit to support the former with his head. As they powdered the pole with dirt, two more men followed. When all four men reached halfway to the top, they wrapped the greasy pole with their arms and legs, sitting on each other's head, to catch their breath. As the first man continued to climb, he lost traction and slid down on his partners, inducing uncontrollable laughter in the crowd. The process was repeated, creating a living totem pole until the man on top reached the coveted prize.

After the event, the president for life, François Duvalier, drove by in a long black car and threw several handfuls of new currency bearing his picture in the air, bringing the crowd to a frenzy. The people picked up the money and ran after the motorcade, screaming "Vive Duvalier! Vive Duvalier!" and leaving behind those who were trampled to death.

While we waited near the park for the crowd to disperse, the cook asked, "Did you see the dead Kamokins on the roadside near the airport?"

"No, I didn't go see them," I answered. She was referring to the five people who were suspected of being communists.

"They were shot dead by the Tontons Macoutes [secret police] and the bodies were dumped near the airport for everyone to see. You should have seen them. They swelled up, grinning in the sun like dead dogs," she said. I began to recall a black dog that was hit by a car and left dead in the middle of the street.

"Are the bodies still there?" I asked, thinking of a dead woman I had seen hanging from a tree behind Ecole du Canada. The students had discovered the body during afternoon recess.

"No, they removed them when the smell was too unbearable. Little boy, don't you ever tell anyone that you don't like Duvalier," she said as we walked back to the house. I already knew that the most effective way to commit suicide was to stand in the middle of the street and shout "A bas Duvalier!"

As I continued to follow the cook, I thought about the time she returned from the market trembling as if she had seen a ghost. She made herself some salted tea to calm her nerves and went to see the cook next door. The two of them were always talking about Kennedys when they got paid at the end of the month.

"You'll never believe what just happened in the tap-tap [small bus] on the way back from the market," she began.

"You can sit down, nobody's home," said the neighboring cook. While the two women sat on the front porch, I squatted down beside them to listen to whatever it was that frightened my grown-ups' cook. "The tap-tap driver drove over a pothole, splashing muddy water on a black car with official license plates. When he realized what he had done, he stopped to apologize. As he was wiping the car with his handkerchief, the Tonton Macoute pulled out his revolver and shot him in the head. He fell like a sack of coal. Everyone got out and ran for their lives," she said, still trembling.

Before long a taxi dropped off the mistress of the house and everyone returned to work.

One day I discovered that Denis had not come home and the car was not there to be washed. Lise and Florence were having dinner without him—something they had never done before.

"Where is Monsieur Denis?" I interrupted the cook, who was talking to the maid next door about someone she knew who was wearing a Kennedy. "She walks in that dress like it's new. I bet you it's really a Kennedy," she said, while I waited patiently for my answer.

"He went à l'étranger [abroad]," she replied. A l'étranger usually meant New York, Paris, or Montreal.

I let out a sigh of relief, because Denis was the only one in the house who wanted to take me to the police station for a beating. "I hope he stays there forever," I whispered to myself.

One midafternoon while sweeping the yard I learned that Kennedy was actually a person rather than another name for articles of used clothing that came from the United States. A neighbor came out and said, "They've just announced on the radio that President Kennedy has been assassinated." Then everyone went about their business as if nothing had happened.

Denis had found a job in New York and was making preparations to send for his family. His second child, a baby boy, was soon born.

The men were coming back to see Florence again. Lise was not happy about the situation and a strain was apparent in their relationship. They avoided each other as much as possible. Lise was leaving with the children to spend time with her mother as much as possible and soon moved out of Florence's house. I returned to school and was kept in the fifth grade due to excessive absences.

Florence had two lovers—a medical student named Paul who seemed much younger than Denis and old man Roland, a government official who was old enough to be Denis's father. His hair was gray and he walked as though he were carrying a heavy load on his shoulder. Old man Roland was paying Florence for her time, usually one hour twice a week on specific days. Paul, tall and heavy, was receiving money from Florence for his time. She was very much in

love with Paul, hoping to marry him to become "Madame Doc-
teur." She prepared special suppers every time he was coming and
made her bed with fresh linen. Of all the men who came to visit
Florence, Paul was the only one who acknowledged me, giving me
a few pennies sometimes. I admired him for the attention and for
saving me from a few beatings.

One evening Paul came to visit while Florence was at the neighbor's house. He brought a plastic soccer ball and gave it to me. I
never felt so excited in my life. My first significant gift! To me, Paul
was both Superman and Batman, the two superheroes who always
made me smile while watching them on television from the back of
the house.

"I want you to tell me something," said Paul.

"What do you want to know?" I asked.

"Does Florence bring other men to her bedroom?" he asked.

I thought about the question for a moment. "Non," I said. Paul
took the ball from my hands.

"I promise that I won't tell her if you tell me the truth," he said,
giving the ball back to me.

"Oui," I whispered.

"How many?" he asked.

"One," I answered.

"When was he here?" he asked.

"Sunday night," I replied.

"Does he give her money?" he asked.

"Oui," I answered.

"Good boy," he said, patting my head.

"Come with me," he said, leading me to Florence's bedroom. Paul
took off all his clothes and began to masturbate. Embarrassed, I
turned my head away to keep from watching him.

"Look, see this. I'm gonna put all of it inside Florence," he told
me. Suddenly, I didn't like him as much. He was no longer my hero.

"Bobby," yelled Florence from the yard. I ran out of the room
with the ball before she called my name a second time.

"Where is Monsieur Paul?" she asked.

"He is in bed," I answered.

"Did he give you the ball?" she asked.

"Oui," I answered.

Florence went inside to see him. She took food and a bottle of Coca-Cola to her room. After Paul had left, Florence called me to her room. She sat in her bed dressed in her kimono, looking disturbed.

"What did you tell Monsieur Paul?" she asked.

"I told him nothing," I answered. She reached for my crotch and held on to my penis with her thumb and index finger.

"What did you tell Monsieur Paul?" she repeated, pinching me harder.

"He asked me if other men come to visit sometimes and I said oui," I replied as tears ran down my face.

"Don't you ever tell him anything again, do you hear me?" she screamed as she continued to pinch and pull.

"Oui," I answered.

"You go to hell, you extrait caca, you little faggot," she yelled as she slapped me across the face with her other hand.

The next time Paul returned, I pretended not to see him.

"Bonjour, Bobby," he said smiling.

Since Florence was listening, I replied "Bonjour" without looking at him. He and Florence went to the bedroom.

Old man Roland had stopped coming to visit, while Paul was showing up for lunch and dinner. It seemed that after every meal he and Florence disappeared into the bedroom. When he couldn't come for lunch, Florence would prepare a picnic basket complete with fruit juice and send me to deliver it to Paul's mother's house, along with a small brown envelope containing money.

Paul's mother, Madame Duval, was the fattest old woman I had ever seen. She reminded me of a huge spinning top. Her upper torso was disproportionately small, but her midsection and hips were huge. She wouldn't get off her chair unless it was absolutely necessary, and when she did it was always with the help of a cane. She took one small step at a time and always had a gauze taped to her left calf. I once heard Florence say to her friend Claudette that Madame Duval's leg would never be healed because a bâca, a bad loa, resided in that leg.

Madame Duval had a boy restavec named Jean. He was as thin as a skeleton with a face full of scars. I never had a chance to speak to him because he had to be constantly by his "owner's" side. Like me, he couldn't speak unless spoken to.

One day Paul was expected for lunch but did not come. Florence appeared upset. She gave me an address along with directions for a house in another neighborhood.

"Go across the street from this house and see if Monsieur Paul's car is parked on the street there."

I followed her directions and found the house. Paul's car was indeed parked on the street. I returned and gave Florence the news.

"His car is there," I told her. She was enraged. Later Paul showed up and tried to embrace an unresponsive Florence. Every time he tried, Florence turned away. After supper, they went to the bedroom. After a while, they both came out smiling at each other. Every time Paul was late, Florence would send me to find out if his car was parked at the same location. Most of the time it was.

"That little whore wants to take my doctor away from me," Florence would say with fiery eyes. Paul took as much money as he could from her and went to Paris to finish medical school.

"We'll get married when I get back," he once told her. Florence's dream of marrying a doctor never came true. She became bitter and took her frustrations out on me at every opportunity.

Florence sold the house and rented an apartment in a townhouse in another city. She began preparations to emigrate to the United States. Occasionally I went to school, but only for the morning session. I was placed in the fifth grade. In the afternoons, I fetched water to keep two huge drums filled for household necessities, because in this new neighborhood the water didn't come regularly. Carrying heavy buckets of water on my head caused my hair to thin on top. Other children called me "restavec tête chauve [bald-headed restavec]."

One Friday morning, Florence sent me to Fruits de Mer, a fish store, with one dollar to buy red snapper. She wanted to prepare a special dinner for Lise, who already had a departure date. It was her way of patching things up with Lise, knowing that she would soon find herself living in New York in Lise's house. When I reached the store, I noticed that my pocket had a hole in it and the money was missing. The store owner recognized me, since I had been coming to his store every Friday.

"Sir, I lost the money. Please give me the fish," I begged.

"No money, no fish," he replied.

"But sir, if I go back without the fish I will be killed. You must give me the fish," I begged again.

"Get out of my store before I throw you out. I think you spent the money on candy," replied the owner.

I began to sob. I dropped to my knees, begging the owner, "Please let me have the fish for the love of God." The owner walked around the counter, grabbed me by the back of my shorts, and threw me out like an unwanted kitten. On my way back home, I stopped by a wall where men always stopped to urinate. A slow breeze carried the powerful stench to my face. Four men approached the wall to relieve themselves. I waited for them to finish. I begged each one for money, explaining that I had a hole in my pocket and that my "grown-up" was going to kill me. "S'il vous plaît [please], monsieur, s'il vous plaît," I sobbed. They ignored me and kept on going. I walked home very slowly with a palpitating heart, hoping never to get there.

As I reached the gate, I looked at the front porch and saw Florence in her rocking chair. Her eyes were full of anger. "What took you so long and where is the fish?" she asked.

"I lost the money," I replied, sobbing and trembling. Florence grabbed me by the ear and led me to the back porch.

"Get on your knees," she yelled, reaching for the broom handle. She kicked me to the ground, placing a foot on my throat while beating me. I could not breathe. It seemed that someone was slowly turning off the light of day and everything that made noise. Lise watched as Florence pounded away. My body went limp and I couldn't feel any pain. A neighbor came out. Realizing that I was not moving, he rushed over and pushed Florence aside. "You're killing him," he shouted.

"He stole my dollar, that little thief," she yelled. For a brief moment, I was floating in the air, watching the man lift me slowly by the piece of rope that served as my belt and force air into my lungs. I soon sat up. He then took me to his apartment and made me rest on the couch. His mother gave me a cup of salted water to drink.

"Poor child, where is your maman?" said the gray-haired woman, nursing my wounds with a cold rag.

"I don't have a maman," I answered grimacing. The substance in the rag stung me. I looked in the mirror against the wall; my face was bumpy and red. The image of René flashed into my mind, but René's face had been worse. Every movement, every cough and sneeze, was painful. The woman took me by the hand and led me outside. Florence was in her rocking chair, rocking slowly back and forth. I never saw her angrier.

"Don't have pity on him, he's a little thief. Not too long ago, he stole milk and tried to replace it with water. He's a con artist who can buy and sell you," said Florence.

"I think he's learned his lesson," replied the aged woman.

"He's a milk seller; he'll do it again," said Florence.

"Get on your knees and ask for forgiveness," said the gray-haired woman.

I slowly bent down and dropped to my knees. With my arms crossed and head hung I said, "Pardon me, I will never lose money again."

"Go away. You will not eat today," said Florence.

The cook was sent to the fish store. Dinner was late and I was not fed. By late evening the doors were locked. Florence and Lise went out together in a taxi. I sat in the yard.

The neighbor called me into her kitchen and gave me a plate of food. Then she heated a dark, thick, smelly oil and massaged my bruised chest and back. That night I slept on the back porch.

Lise soon left for New York to join Denis, and left her children in the care of her mother. Florence was to accompany them to New York as soon as her travel papers were in order. Denis was sending money to his mother-in-law to care for his children, but none to his mother. Florence was getting desperate. She was losing money playing the lottery. She fired the cook. The neighbor's cook went to the market for her and she did her own cooking, probably for the first time.

One evening Florence was making goat-head soup. I handed
her a ladle that she asked for, and she broke it on my head because
it was dirty. I felt a warm liquid oozing down the back of my neck.
I thought it was sweat, but when I wiped it and looked at my hand
I saw blood. The same neighbor who had cared for me before
stopped the bleeding, smashed some green leaves in a small mortar, and tied them on my wound.

Max, an old friend of Florence's, came to visit with a very short
white man late one evening. They sat on the porch for a short
while and then Max left, leaving his companion behind. Florence
moved to the living room with the white stranger. His head came
slightly below her shoulder. Thinking that they were going to
watch television in the living room, I went around the back. As I
stepped on the cement block to look inside, I saw the stranger sitting on the couch while Florence was on her knees, with her head
buried in the stranger's lap. His eyes were closed and his mouth
was open. Sensing that I was not supposed to watch whatever was
going on, I slowly stepped back down and went inside by the
backdoor. I sat in the kitchen, trying to memorize the pages I had
copied from a school friend's textbook earlier that day.

"Bobby," yelled Florence.

"Plaît-il," I answered, rushing before she called me twice.

"Go in the living room and clean the wet spot on the floor,"
she said.

"Oui," I said, rushing to get a rag.

"Why would they spit on the floor?" I asked myself as I cleaned
the floor. The diminutive white stranger had just left.

Max visited more often with men that had never come to visit
before. Each visit was the same as the last. Max never stayed for
more than five minutes, but he always left the visitors behind.

Florence became very ill around this time and kept me home
from school. She quit going to church in the morning. Sometimes
she spent the entire day in bed. She gave me instructions on cooking and making tea. I was constantly by her bed, applying com-
presses to her forehead and wiping her face.

One day she looked at me and said softly, "What would I do

without you?" Her words warmed my heart and made me feel wanted for the first time in my life. I felt proud of myself. She took my hand and held it on her forehead as tears rolled down the side of her sickly brown face. I was frightened. I had never seen her cry before. My lips began to quiver as tears formed and rolled down my face. I thought Florence was dying and wondered, "Where will I go?" I made my bedding on the floor next to her bed, looking in on her as often as I could.

The next morning, her condition deteriorated. I felt her forehead. She was running a high fever and her eyes remained shut. I sautéed a small green onion with tomatoes in olive oil and made soup with stale bread. She would not eat. I was worried. I ran to our previous neighborhood at breakneck speed and went to the clinic. I entered a doctor's office and asked for help. "My maman is very sick—she is dying!" I shouted, tears running down my face.

A doctor recognized me. He was an old friend who had come to Denis's wedding as well as Emilie's baptism. "Who's your maman?" he asked.

"Madame Cadet," I replied.

"Are you the little boy who's staying with her?" he asked.

"Oui, we're living in another neighborhood now," I replied with hurt feelings.

"Let's go," he said, grabbing his black leather bag.

I got in the front seat of his car and gave him directions to the house. The doctor examined Florence and gave her a shot. After a few more visits, she was going to church again. Everything seemed normal.

Then Florence was served with an eviction notice for not paying the rent. The landlord wanted her out immediately. She sold the furniture piece by piece. She was convinced that her sickness as well as her financial troubles were the result of a wanga, a type of black magic charm that Paul's much younger lover had set somewhere for her, and that she had walked over it. She was worshipping her loas again and revenge was on her mind. She was always making some concoctions, putting them in brown paper bags, and sending me to place them at the entrance of Paul's ex-lover's house during the hours of darkness. Since I was always afraid of getting caught, I simply tossed the bags in the nearest pile of garbage I could find.

"Did you do it?" she would ask me upon my return.

"Oui," I would answer.

8 **Yvette, an old girlfriend,** came to visit. She invited Florence to move into her house. She lived in a two-story house, complete with balcony and detached servants' quarters. The family's bedrooms and the bathrooms were on the second floor; the living room, dining room, and kitchen were on the first floor. I liked the move at first, because food was always plentiful.

Yvette had two daughters: fifteen-year-old Jeanne and thirty-six-year-old Anne-Marie, who was married with three girls and a boy about my age. Anne-Marie was also expecting a fifth child. Her husband, Jacques Villard, a tall mulatto, worked for the Haitian government.

Anne-Marie's oldest daughter, sixteen-year-old Catrine, shared a room with her Aunt Jeanne. Six-year-old Véronique shared a room with her nine-year-old sister Cécile, and fourteen-year-old Olivier had a room to himself.

Florence shared Yvette's room. They were as compatible as twins, worshipping the same loas, sharing each other's clothes, and enjoying the same kinds of food. Yvette was tall and majestic like Florence, but darker in complexion. They wore tight dresses and seemed to swing their hips purposely when they walked.

Sophie, the head housekeeper, supervised a laundress and a cook. She controlled all household activities and served as a second mother to the children, but without the power to discipline them.

The very same evening that Florence moved in, Yvette told me to report to Sophie for my duties. I reported to her with my cardboard box and bedding.

"You gonna be sleeping in this room," she said, pointing to a maid's room. It was small and windowless with a cement floor, just big enough for a small bunk. I placed my possessions on the floor.

"I'll wake you up at five-thirty every morning. Your job is to wash Monsieur Villard's car before he goes to work, wash the porch, sweep the yard, fill the tubs for the children, and make sure the bathroom tanks are filled, because sometimes the water pressure is too weak to reach the upstairs," explained Sophie.

"Where is the gardener?" I asked.

"We didn't need him anymore with you staying with us now. What did you think?" asked Sophie.

"My school starts at nine o'clock," I said.

"Forget about school, you won't be going. And know your place. Put 'Monsieur' or 'Mademoiselle' before the children's names and don't eat in the dining room," said Sophie.

I felt discouraged by the news that school was over for me and knew that it was pointless to appeal to Florence.

Olivier had just finished his homework. He wanted to show me his collections of comic books, stamps, and marbles.

"My name is Olivier. What's your name?" he asked.

Before I could answer, Sophie interrupted. "To you his name is Monsieur Olivier. You're a restavec, know your place."

"Don't worry about Sophie, and don't let her scare you," said Olivier.

"My name is Bobby" I said.

"Let's go to my room," said Olivier excitedly.

I looked at Sophie and followed Olivier upstairs to his room.

"I want you to sleep in my room." said Olivier. I smiled in disbelief.

"I can't. I am supposed to sleep in the maid's room," I said.

"I can fix that," said Olivier with an air of confidence.

"How?" I asked.

"Follow me," said Olivier. I followed him upstairs. He walked into his grandmother's room while I waited behind the door.

"Florence?" said Olivier.

"Darling," answered Florence in French. The word *darling* struck me like a knife. I felt like I was drowning in my own blood.

"How can she call him darling and call me extrait caca? He never did anything for her," I said to myself.

"I want Bobby to share my room with me," requested Olivier. Florence was silent, waiting for Yvette to intervene.

"Don't you know who you are?" asked Yvette.

"Oui, I am Olivier," he responded naively.

"Have you looked at him and looked at yourself?" asked Yvette firmly.

"Oui, I looked at him, but why can't he share my room with me?" asked Olivier.

"Ask your mother when she comes home," said Yvette sharply.

"Okay," responded Olivier, walking out. I followed him back to his room.

"Maman will say okay, you'll see," said Olivier, looking at me.

"Bobby, get over here," shouted Florence. I left Olivier and went to Yvette's room.

"I want you to make yourself useful in this house, and don't encourage Monsieur Olivier. Remember, know your place," she said. Yvette looked at me with disgust. I went downstairs to the maid's room.

A car pulled into the driveway. Olivier ran outside.

"Maman, can Bobby sleep in my room?" asked Olivier excitedly.

"Ask your papa," she answered. Anne-Marie and Jacques looked at each other for a moment, and then Jacques said "Okay" reluctantly. Olivier approached me. "It's okay, Papa said it's okay." I collected my cardboard box and bedding from the floor. Sophie gave me a dirty look.

"Monsieur Olivier is not your brother, and don't act like he is, you little restavec," she said disgustedly. Once we were in Olivier's room, he opened my box and pulled out a tin cup, a dented aluminum plate, a few old rags, and two notebooks.

"Is that all you have?" he asked, looking puzzled.

I nodded yes. Olivier looked in his closet and pulled out two pairs of pants and two shirts.

"Try these on," he said. I obeyed. He and I were the same size. Except that I was a shade lighter in complexion. Olivier took the clothes to his mother's room and asked permission to give them to me. He returned and said, "Maman said that you can have them."

"Merci," I said. I now had four shirts and four pairs of pants, an amount I had never had before.

On the other side of the wall, Yvette, Anne-Marie, and her husband, Jacques, were having a meeting. As I was about to lie down, I heard my name called loudly. I jumped to my feet and hurried to Yvette's room.

"Did you tell Monsieur Olivier that you wanted to share his room?" she thundered with fire in her eyes.

"Non," I answered, my heart pounding. Jacques and Anne-Marie went to Olivier's room to have a talk with him.

"You're not allowed to sleep in Monsieur Olivier's room. You understand me?" asked Yvette.

"Oui," I answered. Florence looked at me angrily.

"Motherless son of a bitch, don't you know your place? I don't know why I gave you my name. I am gonna change it to Bobby Joseph instead. Get your things out of Monsieur Olivier's room and go where you belong," said Florence.

I returned to Olivier's room, thinking that I didn't want to have *Joseph* for a last name. I gathered my things and returned to the maid's room. Sophie gave me a repulsive stare.

"I knew somebody was going to put you in your place," she said. I made my bed on the cement floor and went to sleep.

At five o'clock in the morning I was awakened by Sophie, who also discovered that my bedding was wet.

"You little restavec bedwetter. You wanted to sleep in Monsieur Olivier's room? How dare you?" she said. Sophie made me spread the wet rags on a pile of rocks in the back and handed me a bar of laundry soap.

"This is your soap and toothpaste and don't you use anything of mine," she said. I took the soap, scraped my secondhand toothbrush on it, and brushed my teeth. Before breakfast I washed the car, hosed the porch, and swept the yard. Then Sophie ordered me to fill the tubs for the children's baths because the water pressure was too weak to reach the upstairs. I spent the whole morning carrying bucket after bucket of water upstairs on top of my head to fill the tanks every time someone flushed the toilet.

After breakfast, a chauffeur arrived to take the children to school. For me, going to school was out of the question. After I ate, I mopped the dining room floor, cleaned the bathrooms, and dusted the furniture.

I asked Sophie if I could go to school in the afternoon for the math and history classes. She agreed as long as the water pressure was strong enough to reach the bathrooms upstairs and the three huge metal drums used as reservoirs were filled. But it seemed that the pressure was strong only on certain days.

On days when the water did not come at all because the pressure was too low, I fetched water from a nearby ravine to keep the bathroom tanks filled. Weekends were especially tiresome for me, because everyone was home and it seemed that the toilets were constantly being flushed.

Olivier was forbidden to play with me because such fraternization, Yvette feared, might lower his prestige or social standing in the eyes of his peers. But when the water came all day and in full force, I was able to play with Olivier in our secret location near the ravine. Olivier resented it when I called him monsieur but tolerated it to keep his parents—especially Yvette—from getting angry with him. At the secret location, he met with other neighborhood peers to play marbles or war games. After playing, we could not go home together. Olivier made sure that he went home first so that he could ask Sophie loudly, "Where is Bobby?" I would show up just in time to answer, "Here I am, Monsieur Olivier."

The girls kept to themselves all the time. To them I did not exist until they needed something brought to them.

Ecole Simone Duvalier was my new school. It was on the other side of the ravine, poorly kept and unfinished. Only the blackest and the poorest children went there. There were no administrators or counselors. The classes were always overcrowded. Latecomers leaned against the back wall, using their knees to write on their slates.

Some afternoons when I knew I would have to fetch water after school, I would hide my school clothes and notebooks in the bucket. Once I got to the ravine, I'd change, hide my work clothes behind a rock, and carry the bucket to class as a book bag. After school, at four o'clock, I'd go back down in the ravine, change back into my work clothes, and hide my school materials, to be retrieved later, before darkness. I missed the morning sessions when writing, French, and morals were taught. Whenever I had a few moments to myself, I read Olivier's comic books under a lemon tree behind the house.

Sometimes Olivier would carry my school materials under his shirt to the ravine. Once there, he would switch clothes with me and wait for my return. I would laugh at Olivier for having filthy rags and shiny shoes, and he would laugh at me for having good clean tailor-made clothes and no shoes.

Olivier shared whatever he had with me—candy, dessert, and sometimes his allowance. The sharing always took place away from the house.

During the week of Mardi Gras, when the family went to watch the floats in front of the National Palace, I was always left behind with the maids because restavecs were not allowed to ride with the family. I would go in the street and run after *chaloskas*, men in masks and costumes with strings of Coke bottle caps wrapped around their legs for the sound effect. Their three-cornered hats resembled the one worn by the statue of Jean-Jacques Dessalines in Park Champ-de-Mars. I joined other children shouting in Creole, "Chaloska, I am not afraid of you—you are human."

Other masked and costumed men, called *lamayottes*, carried cardboard boxes containing anything from a snake to a white doll. They charged those who were curious enough to pay to see what was inside.

Some women disguised themselves, carrying baskets of leaves on top of their heads to sell. The leaves served no medicinal purposes, but people who wished to hear sexually explicit language called the vendors into their yards. The more the buyers paid, the more they heard.

Before I returned to the house, I watched some small musical bands call *RaRas*. While the men played drums and bamboo tubes, the women sang. I stayed away from them because some people said that they were loups-garous and that they could fly, especially at midnight.

Yvette became suspicious of my friendship with Olivier. She had observed that whenever I was gone, Olivier was missing as well. She resisted the temptation of having us followed, but she always said sarcastically "The two brothers have returned" when she noticed Olivier and me arriving together. That was her way of reminding Florence that I had forgotten my place, and also her way of reminding Olivier that he was doing something that was socially unacceptable.

One early Saturday afternoon while on the balcony, Yvette noticed Olivier and me socializing and playing together behind the house.

"What's going on down there? Bobby, don't you have work to do?" she asked in Creole. "And Olivier, don't you have homework to do?" she asked in French.

We quickly separated. I grabbed a bucket and went to fetch water to fill the toilet tanks and Olivier went inside to do his homework. When I returned with the water, Florence and Yvette were waiting for me. After I filled the tanks, Yvette walked in the bathroom, grabbed my neck from behind, and forced me down to my knees. She lifted the lid and forced my head into the dirty toilet. "This is better than you because it knows its place and you don't know yours," she said, pushing down the flush handle. "See, it's going to its place; now you stay in yours," she added.

My face was wet. As I lifted my head, I blew the dirty water off my lips and dried my face with the tail of my shirt. I looked into Florence's eyes as if to say "How can you let her do this to me?"

Florence was angry. On my way out of the bathroom, she led me to the balcony by the ear. She looked everywhere for something with which to beat me; finally she grabbed a small child's chair and swung it at my head. I held out my hands to protect my face. My little finger was struck and I felt a very sharp pain. Florence was advancing and swinging wildly at me. As I was about to be pinned against the rail, I jumped off the balcony and landed atop a lemon tree that broke my fall to the ground.

Olivier rushed outside and found me leaning against the tree, holding my right hand in pain.

"Are you all right?" he said with sympathy.

"I think my finger is broken," I replied ashamedly. Olivier walked away to keep from being seen with me. Before nightfall my hand was swollen to twice its normal size and the finger was slightly green. Despite the constant throbbing pain, Sophie made sure that I did my chores. Some days the car had to be washed twice, depending on where Monsieur Villard had driven.

Watching the children do their homework and listening to Florence saying "little darling" to them was more painful to me than the injured finger.

On Saturday evenings everyone sat on the front porch. When the bells of the ice cream cart were heard, it was my duty to rush out to the street to summon the vendor into the yard. The children gathered around the cart shouting: "I want chocolate." "I want vanilla." "I want coconut." Then I took the adults' orders and money to the vendor. After I served everyone, I returned the change to Monsieur Villard and sneaked to the back of the house where Olivier was waiting to share his treat with me. He would hold the chocolate cone in front of my mouth, waiting for me to take a bite. I always hesitated, feeling as though I was about to break a law. As we took turns licking an ice cream cone, I felt equal to him. After such moments, whenever I prepared his bath, flushed the toilet after him, or shined his shoes, I felt more like a parent caring for his child than a restavec slaving for food and shelter.

I liked Olivier very much. He was different from other rich boys, breaking every rule of his social class. He bought cooked food from street vendors, befriended children of the very poor, and sometimes sat in the company of the maids when his parents were not home.

One morning I was in Olivier's room returning his shoes after I had shined them. I told him a dirty joke that I had heard from a vendor of leaves. He burst out laughing.

"Olivier, why are you laughing like this?" shouted his mother from the opposite room.

"Bobby's tickling me," he shouted back. Anne-Marie summoned me into the hallway near the bathroom.

"Get on your knees," she snapped. I obeyed her command. My heart was pounding. She then fetched her husband's leather belt from their armoire and began to beat me, saying repeatedly, "Don't you ever tickle Monsieur Olivier again." I begged for mercy, telling her that Monsieur Olivier was lying. She only became angrier. Olivier came to my rescue, "No Maman, Bobby was not tickling me. I said that because he told me a joke," he said. Anne-Marie did not believe Olivier. She continued beating me. After my punishment, Florence came out of her room and said to me disgustedly, "Chien, sang sale [you dirty-blooded dog]."

By the spring of that year, Anne-Marie was believed to be nearly ten months pregnant. While her medical doctor had advised her to be patient and said that she would deliver at any time, she consulted a mambo, a practitioner of voodoo, who told her that an enemy had tied the baby inside her stomach. Everyone in the family was concerned. Voodoo priestesses were coming in and out of the house, there to conduct ceremonies. They rubbed Anne-Marie's stomach with concoctions designed to untie the unborn. These priestesses went into trances and spoke with deep masculine voices. At times, three to four different personalities appeared in the same person. They identified themselves as Dambala, Papa Legba, Ogun, and Erzulie Yeux Rouges.

Florence too sometimes became possessed, but always by the same loa—Ogun.

The enemy who had tied the unborn was probably the mistress of Anne-Marie's husband, suggested the mambo.

One late morning after breakfast, a huge dark-brown butterfly flew into the house. One of the children shouted, "Look at this big butterfly." Florence saw it and announced that it was a bad spirit sent by the enemy. The maids were ordered to chase it out of the room. Everyone panicked. While the children were kept inside for their own protection, I was told to continue fetching water. I became paranoid, thinking that a loup-garou would kill me or suck my blood on my way to the ravine. One of the maids started to sing incomprehensible words. Yvette, who wanted to know if the maid's loa had come to warn her about something, guided her upstairs to her bedroom. The maid started to dance as though every part of her body was possessed by a different being. Her reaction to the butterfly convinced everyone in the house that someone indeed was out to harm Anne-Marie's unborn baby.

The children were lectured on the danger of picking up objects from the ground. The house was like a fort under siege. On another occasion, a small bird flew in. Again everyone panicked. This time, Florence ordered the maids to capture it alive. They closed all the windows and chased the bird with brooms and pillowcases throughout the house until it was captured. Florence summoned her loa and began to talk with a deep voice. Within the hour, the mambo came to visit. She was to decide the fate of the bird. A big voodoo ceremony took place in Yvette's room. Red and black hand-dipped candles were lit in front of an open cabinet decorated with supernatural images in a corner of the room. The maid who had been singing summoned another loa and began to dance like a snake, crawling on her stomach while her arms remained at her sides. The mambo and Florence's loa gave instructions to Yvette, who ordered me to bring a pail of water into her bedroom. A concoction was made with several different leaves and other ingredients and poured into the pail of water. Anne-Marie disrobed and stepped in it, and Yvette rubbed her stomach with the leaves, presumably to untie the unborn and chase away bad spirits. Then one by one the children were called in to be washed.

"There is one other child that needs to be bathed," said the loa in Florence's head.

"Where is Bobby?" yelled Yvette.

I, who was standing behind the door, quickly appeared. "Here I am," I said, looking into Florence's bloodshot eyes. She was humming and swinging her head slowly from side to side. Beads of sweat, inching from beneath her black wig to her brown face, met collectively at her chin before dripping down the front of her red blouse. Yvette looked at me as if my presence was offensive to her.

"Take off your clothes and get in the pail," snapped Yvette. I slowly undressed, covered my private parts with my injured hand, and stepped into the cold green smelly liquid. "Well, don't just stand there. Wash yourself," commanded Yvette. With my good hand I reached down, took a fistful of wet leaves, and rubbed myself up and down until I was entirely wet. Goose bumps soon covered my skin. The mambo, who spoke in a deep nasal voice, walked over to me, reached down, and took my injured hand in hers. I quickly covered myself with my good hand.

"You have a bad hand," she said. I lifted my head and looked at Florence again.

"He's a good boy," said the mambo, as she closed my little finger firmly in her hand. I grimaced—the pain was unbearable. After a while she opened her hand. "You can get dressed now. Your finger's going to be fine," she said. I put on my clothes and walked out. Before the week ended, I had the full use of my hand.

That night Anne-Marie's water broke. Monsieur Villard drove her to the hospital. By late evening, she had a ten-pound baby boy.

9 **Florence had a departure date.** She bought suitcases and had several dresses made. She was very excited, but I was worried. I had no idea what was going to happen to me, and I didn't want to be abandoned in the streets like other restavecs who were no longer wanted. Two of my restavec friends had been released into the streets to fend for themselves. Their "owners" had sold their house and moved à l'étranger—to New York. They didn't even try to find the families of their slave children and they didn't even say good-bye.

I had diarrhea and was wetting my bed every night. Florence had stopped beating me after the balcony incident. It would have been very inconvenient for her to go to the maid's room in the middle of the night. Besides, the maid's room was locked from the inside.

Every morning Sophie gave me some disinfectant with which to rid the room of the urine odor.

I was dying to ask Florence what was going to happen to me, but every time I went near her the words could not escape my tongue. So I asked Olivier to find out for me.

"What did she say?" I asked.

"She said that she's thinking of something, and I asked Maman if we could keep you and she said no," replied Olivier. I was devastated. I ran to the bathroom. For days I had no appetite and spent sleepless nights wondering about my fate.

On the eve of Florence's departure, a brown Jeep wagon pulled up in front of the house. A medium-built white man stepped out.

He looked at me and nodded hello. "Bonjour, Monsieur," I said nervously. It was my father, my third time to see him.

Florence had been expecting him, apparently to discuss my fate. She sat in the living room with him for a good ten minutes, and then Philippe walked out without saying good-bye to me. Tears filled my eyes as I watched the Jeep disappear in the distance.

"That was Philippe Sébastien. I didn't know he was a friend of Florence's," said Olivier.

"Yes, he is my papa," I said, drying off my face.

"His twins go to my school," said Olivier.

"I don't know them," I said.

"They have a car and they drive to school," added Olivier excitedly.

Later, at bedtime, I thought that as soon as Florence left, Anne-Marie might ask me to leave. I stayed up all night wondering about my fate.

The day of Florence's departure arrived. Her flight to New York was to depart at four o'clock in the afternoon. My heart felt like it was fighting to leave my body. By two o'clock Denis's children arrived with their grandmother. They were happy to see me. I played with them until it was time to go.

Three cars were waiting to take Florence to the airport. "Bobby, take the luggage to the car," said Yvette. Trembling with nervousness, I placed the suitcases in the trunks of the cars. Florence sat in the backseat of Monsieur Villard's car with the children. Anne-Marie sat next to her husband. Everyone else piled in the two other cars. My lips began to quiver and my eyes were watery. As the cars drove off, Florence waved at me. I ran after the cars shouting, "Maman, Maman! Please don't leave me!" Walking back to the house, Florence's voice echoed in my mind, "You'll never be anything but a shoeshine boy." Suddenly I realized that I wouldn't have money to buy the supplies needed to shine shoes when Anne-Marie asked me to leave.

The maids were laughing at me as I ran behind the cars, and they spent the rest of the evening teasing me. "Don't you know by now that blood is thicker than water?" said one maid.

"It doesn't matter how long you've been with her, you're a

restavec. Her grandchildren will always come first," said another. I ignored them both. I made my bed and lay down.

By late evening I heard Monsieur Villard's car in the driveway. My heart began to pound. "I hope that they will change their minds and let me stay." I whispered. At daybreak I awoke with a plan. I thought that if I worked as hard as I could, Anne-Marie would let me stay. So I washed the car as best I could, swept the yard, and mopped the entire first floor. Then I went upstairs and cleaned the bathrooms. After I finished my chores, I went to see Sophie.

"Sophie, please speak to Madame Villard for me. Tell her how useful I am and that I will work very hard for her," I said.

"They're getting rid of you because you don't know your place. You keep playing with Monsieur Olivier like he was your brother," said Sophie.

"Please, speak to her for me. I will not play with Monsieur Olivier again," I begged, sobbing uncontrollably.

"I have work to do. Get away from me," said Sophie, walking away.

After breakfast Sophie handed me an old pair of Olivier's shoes.

"Here. If they're too big, stuff them with paper. Put some clean clothes on and pack your box," she said.

"Where am I going?" I asked, shaken.

"You're going to Petite Rivière to live with Madame Cadet's sister," said Sophie.

I tried on the shoes. They were too big. I stuffed them with pieces of rags to make them fit and changed into clean clothes—a pair of khaki shorts and an old shirt of Olivier's.

"Go say good-bye," said Sophie. I went inside. Anne-Marie and Yvette were sitting on the balcony. I stood in front of them with head down and arms crossed against my chest.

"I am leaving now," I said, trembling.

"Good-bye, young man. Take care of yourself," said Anne-Marie.

"Okay, Bobby, good-bye," said Yvette nonchalantly. The children were not home.

When I came out of the house, a taxi was waiting to take me to the bus station. Sophie told the driver to make sure that I got on the right bus, to Petite Rivière, and gave me the money. "This is for the taxi and the bus driver," she said. I got in the backseat, holding my box in my lap. "Good-bye, Sophie," I said, avoiding eye contact with her.

"Good-bye, Bobby," she said.

When the taxi reached the bus station, the driver told me to get out and look for a bus named God Is Great.

"If you don't know how to read, ask someone," he said.

"I know how to read," I answered, paying him.

The bus station was a huge unpaved muddy lot. Piles of foulsmelling garbage, swarming with flies, seemed to be everywhere. Street vendors were peddling fabric, unwrapped bread, sugarcane, pots and pans, colorful dresses, shirts, sandals, bottles of fruit juice, and cola.

The buses were huge flatbed trucks, fitted with benches and painted in bright colors. The tops were overly loaded with huge baskets and trunks. Carrying my cardboard box tightly, I walked in front of the parked buses, looking over the windshield of each, searching for the one with the name God Is Great.

I read the names: In the Name of God, Jesus Marie Joseph, God Is Everywhere, St. Jacques, St. Vierge Marie, St. Joseph, God Is My Copilot, God Is Good, St. Antoine, St. Michel, Notre Dame du Cap, and Ave Maria. When I spotted God Is Great, I climbed aboard and sat quietly at the end of a bench, imagining myself walking the streets and carrying a shoeshine box as I made musical tunes by ringing a small bell. At precisely noon, the driver collected money from the passengers and left Port-au-Prince. After a long drive, the road began to get bumpy, causing the passengers to lean from side to side and bounce in their seats.

Going through several small villages of small mud huts, the driver sometimes stopped to drop off passengers or to avoid hitting cows, goats, or donkeys.

Naked children—black as coal with runny noses, white eyes, and protruding stomachs—waved hello or good-bye in clouds of dust, stirred by the thundering muffler. At one stop, some passengers bought cooked food served on green banana leaves from roadside vendors. Some ate with their fingers while others shared a spoon, shaking it off as they passed it around. They drank from bottles and small calabashes and wiped their mouths with the backs of their hands. I bought nothing, although the smell of fried green onions seemed to cause my stomach to growl.

As the bus began to move again, the smell of food and diesel fumes caused me to be sick. In a cold sweat, I hung my head outside to vomit. No one paid any attention to me.

By six o'clock, I began to recognize familiar landmarks. Florence's sister and mother lived minutes away from the huge stone church in the town square of Petite Rivière. Four years earlier, Florence had brought me to spend two weeks with her mother, a kind-hearted elderly woman whom everyone called Grannie Alcée. She had a bad left leg that caused her to walk with a limp. I was eager to see her again because the two weeks I had spent with her were the best times I had ever had. She made sure that no harm came to me, even when I wet my bedding. When neighbors dropped off their babies for Grannie to watch, she would sometimes put the infants to her breast, where they pacified themselves with her nipple.

I thought about her house. It was a two-room stucco cabin with a tin roof, cement floor, large front porch, and two indigo-blue doors. In the attic, she stored sacks of paddy rice, unripened avocados, and mangos. The backyard was a small farm. Her private vegetable garden, on the east side of the house, was meticulously kept. The kitchen, a small mud hut covered with straw, was a stone's throw from the small back porch. A cemented and covered water well was in the west side of the house. In the center of the huge yard was a deep green arbor loaded with bunches of sweet red grapes. Colorful hummingbirds danced in silence over deep red flowers of hibiscus near a bed of white stones. From the branches of two leafless trees hung hundreds of ears of dried corn in rings of barbed wire. In the distance near the outhouse were pens for pigs and goats. Two donkeys and a mule rested near a bush. Chickens walked freely in search of seeds to share with their newly hatched chicks. A big brown dog lay lazily waiting for the smell of food before it would move.

When I had visited, Grannie Alcée had neither refrigerator nor radio, not even a clock. Every meal was cooked over firewood, and she kept track of time by reading shadows on the ground.

The thought of Grannie brought a smile to my face. I remembered the time on my previous visit when early one morning, before the roosters began to crow, I was awakened by the urge to use the outhouse. Everyone was sleeping soundly. I slowly unhooked the door latch and stepped outside. It was dark and I was frightened. Unable to see the outhouse in the distance from where I stood, I squatted beside the house near Grannie's garden, relieved myself, and went back to bed. Before long, I was awakened by familiar noises of morning activities and the strong aroma of Grannie's coffee. I lay worried, thinking about what I had done, because Grannie took pride in maintaining a clean yard. Every morning before she swept around the kitchen hut, she drew water from the well and sprinkled the yard with it to kill the dust.

Before breakfast that particular morning, she assembled all the children beside the house. She had covered my bodily waste with a pile of leaves. "I want to know who relieved himself beside the house this morning," she said, straight-faced. Everyone remained quiet. My heart was palpitating, for I was certain that Grannie would cut a switch from the nearest tree and whip whoever it was. "I want whoever did this to take the shovel, scoop it up, and throw it away," she repeated, pointing to the pile of leaves. When she noticed that the culprit was not about to reveal himself, she reached down and pulled a handful of red hot peppers from her garden and threw them on the pile of leaves. "I will burn these hot peppers with this caca [excrement] and say three words on it. And when the owner of this caca tries to relieve himself again, his intestine will burn like it's on fire and come out of his derrière. Then I'll know who did this," she said angrily. The thought of having my intestine coming out of my derriere frightened me more than the possibility of being whipped.

As she was about to strike a match, I began to cry. I raised my hand in fear and said, "Grannie, I am the one who did this. Please don't burn it." Grannie smiled broadly and toothlessly and said,

"Next time you have to go in the dark, wake up a grown-up or use the chamber pot beside my bed." Grannie cupped my face in her hands affectionately and said, "Don't cry and never lie to me. I have my ways of finding out the truth."

Grannie believed in the power of loas, although she did not have a voodoo shrine. She also believed that every body of water—from rivers to springs to water wells—has a spirit or a *maître*.

In a corner of the house, she kept drinking water in a big clay jar called a *canarie*. Behind the *canarie* was a big bottle containing long, thick leeches the color of red clay, moving about in liquid. Sometimes Grannie would sit in her rocking chair under the *kénèpe* tree and support her swollen left leg with another chair. Then she would strategically place a few leeches on the swollen leg. When a leech reached the size of a small cucumber, she would unhook it and then gently roll it back and forth between her hands to squirt out the dark blood from its sucker.

When the driver stopped, I jumped off with my box. I looked in every direction and suddenly noticed that the bus was the only motor vehicle in town. There was silence. It seemed that the whole town was sleeping except for a few people on horseback and donkeys, returning home from the town square market. After walking a few blocks, I recognized the double blue doors facing the unpaved street. Since they were closed, I found my way to the backyard.

I was shocked. The kitchen roof had a big hole in it, the arbor was missing, and the cemented edge of the water well was badly damaged. There were no animals anywhere to be found. The flowers and the vegetable garden were missing as well.

From where I stood, I noticed that the backdoor was open and flies were buzzing in and out of the house. As I walked in, a powerful stench of urine and human excrement assaulted my nose. Grannie Alcée was lying in her mahogany bed, staring at the ceiling. Her eyes were deep in their sockets and her face looked like a giant dried prune with a hole in the middle of it. Her white hair clung to her head like Spanish moss dangling from a dead branch.

I was devastated. I held my breath as long as I could. "Grannie Alcée?" I called, waving the flies off her face. I called again: "Grannie Alcée?"

She slowly turned her head toward me. "Gertrude!" she said. "Non, Grannie, I am Bobby. Gertrude is not here," I said. Grannie apparently had no recollection of me. Gertrude was her older daughter, Florence's sister. I walked out of the house, filled my lungs with fresh air, and went to the spot where the arbor used to be. I thought about Grannie making coffee, cornbread cakes, sweet potatoes boiled in goat's milk, and scrambled eggs for breakfast.

My fondest memory of Grannie's yard was of the day she had one of her pigs slaughtered. She had sent word a week in advance to a butcher who lived in a faraway village. On a crisp Saturday morning, two butchers with shoulder bags arrived on a big brown mule. One man displayed a variety of sharp knives and daggers and the other produced a small calabash bowl filled with finely chopped garlic, parsley, hot peppers, and green onions. Every dog in the village seemed to have known in advance about the killing of the pig, because they were all present. Children of every age and size were eager to assist. The large, fat, uncooperative pig was wrestled down by the butchers and tied to a table made from a door supported by two chairs. The animal was then washed with the help of the children. A bucket was placed on the ground, under its neck to catch every drop of blood. Nearby a huge bonfire burned in a pit for the removal of the quills. As one butcher pressed down on the head of the squealing pig, the other plunged a long sharp dagger in its throat. All the children reached for the waving curly tail, thinking their efforts would stop the huge animal from budging. The blood was spiced, made into sausages, and served with scrambled eggs for lunch. Dogs fought for scraps while everyone ate, sitting on a long bench under the arbor. Most of the meat was sent to market, but portions were preserved in a barrel with rock salt for daily consumption.

Every day before the big afternoon meal, the neighbor, Madame Emile, who was pregnant with her third child, sent over a bowl of food. One particular meal I liked was eggplant cooked with pork over white rice on one side and red bean sauce on the other. After Grannie Alcée shared the food with the children, she washed the bowl and placed it in the dish basket on the rock pile near the water well to dry. Later Grannie reciprocated with chicken gumbo and sweet potatoes in the same sky-blue crockery bowl whose owner I never knew. When the midwife was delivering Madame Emile's baby, Monsieur Emile Dorsaintville waited nervously under the arbor with their two small children, 'Tit homme (Little Man) and Demi-femme (Half-Woman). The children had been given these names because they had been born abnormally small. After delivery, Madame Emile called the new baby girl, who was born smaller than Demi-femme, Nanpoint-femme (There's No-Woman). Her husband placed the afterbirth in a hole behind their house and planted a banana tree over it to ensure long life for the new arrival.

My reminiscing was soon interrupted.

"Who the devil are you?" said a woman in a patterned dress, large straw hat, and leather sandals. It was Gertrude. In four years, she seemed to have aged twenty years.

"I am Bobby, Aunt Gertrude, remember me?" I answered.

"I don't know any Bobby. Are you here to rob me?" she babbled. The smell of her breath forced me to move back two steps. She was three shades lighter than Florence and much thinner. Florence was always jealous of her light skin and long hair. "If I had your skin color, I'd be a very rich woman," Florence had told her four years earlier.

Gertrude went inside to see Grannie. A short time later Chelaine, Gertrude's adult daughter, arrived with a hand basket. She brought two crockery bowls of cooked food. She recognized me immediately and asked several questions without waiting for answers.

"When did you get here? Did you come by yourself? Did Aunt Florence go à l'étranger?" She went inside and lit the gas lamp. I followed her and waited outside by the door. Gertrude had collapsed in a small bed next to Grannie's. Chelaine came back out, drew water from the well, carried it inside, and gave Grannie a bath. She then changed the sheets and fed her grandmother like a two-year-old child. She gave me her mother's portion of the food.

"What happened to the yard, the animals, and the arbor?" I asked.

"Léon was arrested and killed by the gendarmes three years ago. He was sent on a political killing by someone who had promised him a good job in government. When Grannie heard the news, she suffered a stroke. Then my mother started drinking. She sold everything, even the furniture, to buy tafia [rum]. She's been drunk on tafia ever since," Chelaine explained with teary eyes.

Léon was Gertrude's older son. He had been in his late twenties. Gertrude had invested a lot in his education, hoping he would someday take care of her financial needs. But I remembered him as a thief who used to steal from Grannie's small money sack. Léon used to reach into Grannie's bra, grab the small money sack, and run.

"When did Aunt Florence go à l'étranger?" she asked.

"She left Saturday," I answered.

"Will she send for you?" she asked.

"I don't know. She didn't say," I answered.

"Does your papa know that you're here?" she asked.

"I don't know," I said. Chelaine knew that my father was paying Florence to take care of me and assumed that Florence had been treating me like a son instead of a restavec.

"Simon should be here soon. He'll be very happy to see you," she said. I nodded. Simon was Gertrude's youngest child. He was in his mid-twenties. He had visited Florence in Port-au-Prince a few years earlier. The visit lasted nearly two weeks. Every night he would go to my bedding, pull off his pants, and rub his genitals against my body. He was aware that I was being treated like a restavec and also knew that I was not allowed to talk to Florence until I was addressed. He didn't worry about my telling anyone.

"If you tell anyone, I'll say that it was your idea," he had told me. I thought Simon was disgusting, and I was not looking forward to seeing him. Simon was always trying to kill a hummingbird, called *wanganégresse* in Creole, meaning "magic potion for women." He wanted to dry the dead bird in the sun, grind it into a fine powder, and throw it at beautiful women. Every time he saw a beautiful young girl, he would say, "If I only had some wanganégresse powder."

"Why don't you live here, so you can take care of Grannie?" I asked.

"I sew all day to make a living. If I don't work, everyone in this house will starve. Simon is an apprentice to a shoemaker. Whatever he makes, he keeps for himself. And when he makes nothing, I feed him," Chelaine explained.

Suddenly, I thought about being a shoeshine boy, the profession Florence had chosen for me. Florence's voice echoed in my mind again: "You'll never be anything but a shoeshine boy." Petite Rivière was the wrong place to be a shoeshine boy. The majority of people walked either barefoot or in sandals. The door opened. It was Simon.

"Who is this?" he asked.

"It's Bobby," answered Chelaine. Simon walked toward me and patted my head.

"Hey, Bobby, how are you doing? When did you get here?" he asked.

"Fine. This afternoon," I answered abruptly, giving him a cold stare. Chelaine felt my coldness toward Simon. She looked puzzled.

"I have to get back now. I'll see you tomorrow," she said, leaving.

"What's in the box?" asked Simon.

"My clothes," I replied. Simon opened the box and searched it.

"Do you have any money?" he asked.

"Non," I answered, thinking of the two gourdes in my pocket. Sophie had given me extra money for lunch.

"You sleep on the mat; the divan is mine," said Simon.

I opened a straw mat on the cement floor and sat down. I was still hungry. In a corner were two clay *cruches*, or pitchers, of water. I took out my tin cup from the box and poured myself a drink. I could barely see the water in the dimly lit room—it tasted swampy and fishy.

"I am taking the lamp to the outhouse," I said.

"There is a full moon and there is no outhouse. It was destroyed," replied Simon.

"I need to go to the bathroom," I said.

"Go in the bushes in the back," said Simon.

As I walked out to go relieve myself against a tree in the back-yard, I remembered a particular Sunday afternoon about four years earlier. Simon had on clean clothes and was in a hurry to go see two local soccer teams play a match in an open field. Suddenly the constant echoing cries of a baby were heard far out in the back-yard. Everyone rushed toward the outhouse. The door had been left wide open. The cries were coming from the deep dark smelly hole. Gertrude lit a handful of dried corn husks and held her torch through the hole in the bench, searching for the source of the cries. "Jesus Marie Joseph, it's one of my baby goats. It's buried in caca [excrement]—I can only see its head sticking out. Simon, you left the door wide open—you go down there and get the goat," thundered Gertrude.

"No, Maman, please don't make me go down in there," cried Simon.

"I can sell that goat for four gourdes. May lightning strike me and the Virgin Marie pierce my eyes, you're going down to get the goat," shouted Gertrude. Using the flat end of an ax, Simon re-moved the bench, then tied a rope around the wooden beam. As he was about to descend, Gertrude ordered him to get undressed. "You better take off your clothes. I am not washing them when you get back up," said Gertrude. Simon descended in the nude while everyone waited under a nearby tree. A while later Simon emerged, grimacing and holding the goat against his chest with one hand and covering his private parts with the other. He and the goat were covered with feces. "Go wash yourself in the pigpen," ordered Gertrude. After Simon cleaned himself off in the pig's trough, he went swimming in the Artibonite Canal while Gertrude gave the goat a bath.

When I went back inside, I found Simon in bed in his under-wear and wearing his shoes. I lay down in a fetal position with my back toward him. Simon blew out the lamp. I was disoriented by the thickness of the dark. After a long moment Simon asked, "Are you awake?" I did not answer. "I know you're not sleeping. Hey, do you remember what we used to do when I went to visit Aunt Flor-ence in Port-au-Prince?" he continued. I pretended to be asleep. I heard Simon get off the divan and crawl on his hands and knees toward me. I was deathly frightened. I felt Simon's hands pulling off my shorts. I screamed at the top of my lungs and kicked. Simon quickly found his way back to his bed. He laughed loudly; then all was peaceful.

I was awakened by the crowing of roosters. The bottom of my feet felt sore. Rats had chewed my heels raw. I lay still until the rays of the sun found a few cracks in the wooden shuttered windows. The smell of Grannie's coffee was noticeably missing. I felt crushed by the weight of disappointment.

Someone opened the backdoor. It was Gertrude. I scraped my toothbrush on my soap and went outside with a cup of water to brush my teeth. Simon had no toothbrush. He dipped his wet finger in ashes from the kitchen, scrubbed his teeth, and rinsed his mouth.

"Bonjour, Aunt Gertrude," I said. She seemed surprised to see me. She looked sick and malnourished. Her front teeth were missing and her eyes were bloodshot. She poured water into her hand from a cup and washed her face.

"How are you?" she answered with a smile that could have frightened a small child. I avoided her as much as possible because she was always talking to herself out loud.

Chelaine arrived with a basket. She brought bread soup with tomatoes and coffee. She fed Grannie and returned to her house with me. Chelaine lived in a one-room mud house with a straw roof and dirt floor that was big enough for her bed, a small table, and two chairs. The kitchen, away from the house, was four poles with a roof of two rusted sheets of metal. She had no outhouse and no water well.

She served me a plate of corn flour cooked with okra, tomatoes, and pieces of salted pork. After a while, Simon arrived. He went directly to the kitchen, served himself in a small calabash bowl, and ate outside, leaning against the wall. Then came Gertrude. After she served herself, she ate in the makeshift kitchen, sitting on a log.

Chelaine pulled out her sewing machine from under her bed and began to work. Simon and Gertrude left as soon as they finished eating. Chelaine had no radio, no newspaper, no magazines, no books—not even a clock. A gas lamp sat in the center of a small wooden table. I spent the day with her, holding the fabric when she had to cut. When she thought it was noon, she stopped sewing and began to cook. She placed a pot of dried beans over three rocks, dropped in a piece of aged pork fat, and lit the firewood under it. A woman carrying a hand basket came to pick up a child's dress. She handed Chelaine a small bag of foodstuffs.

When dinner was done, a tall and very dark-skinned man arrived. Chelaine introduced me as the son of Blanc Philippe. His name was Antoine. She served him at the table, while she and I ate outside in the makeshift kitchen, sitting on firewood. Afterward Chelaine asked me to leave. "I'll see you later when I go feed Grannie," she said. I was still hungry.

Instead of going to Grannie's, I went for a walk, looking for fruit trees and watching farmers on horseback returning to their farms from the market. Before darkness fell, I went swimming in the Artibonite Canal and returned to Grannie's yard. I sat on the edge of the water well with my head down, visualizing a healthy Grannie Alcée. The moon was full, the yard was empty, and my chest felt hollow inside. I thought about how everyone used to sit in a circle outside until bedtime, eating roasted corn, making up *cric-crac* riddles, and telling traditional stories about loups-garous and two friends called Bouki and Malice.

Chelaine and Antoine were *placé*, a socially acceptable arrangement in which a man provides a woman with a house and she in return behaves as if she were his wife—probably a legacy left behind by the grands blancs who used to maintain mulatto slaves as concubines. Most married men had such an arrangement. Single men with resources were sometimes *placé* with two to three women. Most wives accepted the practice because they had some financial control over their husband's affairs.

 Before the end of the week, I asked Chelaine if I could live with her instead of sleeping at Grannie's.

"Why?" she asked.

"I can't sleep over at Grannie's because when Aunt Gertrude gets drunk she tries to beat me," I explained. It was easy to escape Gertrude, but fighting off Simon's advances every night was harder than fighting off wild pigs and dogs in the underbrush. I didn't want to accuse Simon of trying to molest me for fear that he might retaliate. After all, he was a man and I was just a boy. Besides, telling Chelaine would not have stopped him.

"This is not my house. I will speak to Antoine and let you know what he says," said Chelaine.

"I will write to my papa in Port-au-Prince and ask him to send you money to take care of me," I added. I was determined not to spend another night at Grannie's. Suddenly Chelaine's eyes lit up.

"In that case, I am certain that it will be all right with Antoine," she said.

I had no idea where in Port-au-Prince my father lived. A few minutes later, Antoine arrived.

"Bobby, why don't you wait outside while I talk to Antoine," suggested Chelaine. I went to the back of the house and listened to their conversation under an open window. At first Antoine said no because the house was too small. When she told him about my writing to Blanc Philippe to get money, he agreed as long as the money was given to him directly. As soon as the conversation ended, I ran back to the front of the house.

"When are you going to write to Blanc Philippe?" asked Antoine smiling.

"Tomorrow morning," I answered, not knowing how or by whom to send a letter to Port-au-Prince. Besides, I had never written a letter before.

"You can stay," he said. I ran to Grannie's house and retrieved my box and the mat. When it was time for bed, Chelaine made a curtain with a bed sheet to separate her bed from my mat. The sounds of their lovemaking kept me awake until Antoine went home to his wife.

In the morning when Simon came for breakfast, I asked him if there was a school in town that I could go to.

"Yes, but it's not free," answered Simon.

"Can you take me there? I want to see it," I said.

"Where will you get money to pay for school? You're wasting your time," he said.

"I'll write to Blanc Philippe and he'll send me the money," I replied.

After breakfast, I followed Simon to town. He pointed to a school and continued on his route. I stopped in front of the gate and read "Ecole Jean-Charles" written on a wooden sign. I looked in the yard and noticed a big brown horse in the distance tied to a pole near an outhouse. A few chickens were scratching for seeds nearby. Since it was Saturday, I didn't expect to see students. There were three small mud houses with straw roofs and abnormally large windows standing side by side. Close to the gate was a bigger house with open windows and a large front porch.

I opened the long wooden gate wide enough to get inside. I was nervous. A big yellow dog, wagging its tail in a friendly way, was looking at me. Out of the house came a tall, robust black man. His bright red shirt was tucked neatly in his well-pressed dark-blue jeans. From his wide, shiny black belt hung a holster, stuffed with a slightly rusted revolver. The reflection of the sun was visible on his black knee-high boots.

"What can I do for you?" he asked in a baritone voice.

"I want to come to school," I answered.

"Where did you go to school before?" he asked.

"Ecole Simone Duvalier in Port-au-Prince," I replied, clearing my voice.

"What grade?" he asked.

"Eighth grade," I answered, knowing that I had never passed the fifth grade due to excessive absences.

"It's three gourdes [sixty U.S. cents] per month. The first month must be paid in advance and I don't take crétins [idiots]," he explained.

"I don't have any money, but I can work for you after school," I said.

"Ha, ha, ha!" He laughed until tears formed in his eyes. He pulled out a red handkerchief and wiped his face. I smiled—I was no longer nervous.

"What about books? You've got to have books," he said.

"I'll borrow books from students and copy the pages," I answered, causing him to laugh again. Florence's voice echoed in my head: "Borrow books and copy the pages."

"Follow me," he ordered. I followed him to the first small hut. He pulled open the squeaky door, walked inside, and opened the windows. Inside were student desks with inkwells, a small table, and a large faded blackboard. The smell of the class-hut was familiar to me.

"I'll give you a dictation and if you make less than ten mistakes, I will accept you," he said. Suddenly my heart began to pound. I was nervous again. I nodded yes and stood in front of the blackboard. The man took a book from the table and opened it. I felt droplets of sweat running down my back. My fingers were moist. My hand trembled as I picked up a piece of chalk from the edge of the faded blackboard. After I wrote the word "Dictée" at the very top, he read aloud the title, "Le Braconnier [The Poacher]." I took a deep breath, lifted my head, and began to write. I retained the phrases as though each was a password on which my life depended, while my hand transferred them to the blackboard to be recognized. "Deux coups tirés. . . . Il lève la tête, le canon d'un revolver braqué sur lui, jette dans la nuit une petite lueur [Two shots fired. . . . He raises his head, the barrel of the revolver, pointed at him, throws into the night a faint glimmer]." At the end of the last phrase, I made a period and stepped back. The man read the dictation again, at times raising his voice to emphasize certain words while I checked for errors. As he approached the board, I handed him the chalk and looked into his eyes. As he began to underline misspelled words, I felt my heart climbing to my throat.

"You've made six mistakes," he said. I relaxed. "Can you analyze the first sentence grammatically?" he asked. I let out a sigh of relief and identified the parts of speech.

"My name is Maître Jean-Charles. What is your name?" he asked.

"My name is Jean-Robert Cadet," I answered.

"I'll see you Monday morning at eight o'clock," said Maître Jean-Charles.

I walked out of the small class-hut, looking at the oinking pigs in the distance near the outhouse, the horse, and the water well nearby. As soon as I reached the street and was out of Maître Jean-Charles' sight, I jumped up and down frantically with excitement, saying, "I am accepted! I am accepted!" I could not wait to share the news with Chelaine. As I reached her house, I ran toward her.

"Aunt Chelaine! Aunt Chelaine! I got accepted to Maître Jean-Charles' school," I said.

"Uh-huh," she said nonchalantly as she turned the handle of her sewing machine.

"Did you write to your papa?" she asked.

"Oui," I answered, leaving the house for a walk through nearby farm villages searching for fallen mangos, avocados, and other fruits to supplement my diet. Once again I found nothing. I was hungry and my stomach felt like it had a knot in it. On my way back to Chelaine's, I noticed a small group of people in a yard, sitting in a circle and singing. I walked up and noticed that they were shelling a basketful of dried ears of corn. Everyone was barefoot.

"Bonjour, messieurs, dames," I said.

"Bonjour," they answered in unison. Everyone was staring at me inquisitively. The smell of food was coming out of a small kitchen hut near the water well. I wanted two corncobs with which to make popcorn but was too ashamed to ask.

"I enjoy shelling corn. May I help?" I asked nervously.

"You can help if you want," said a woman in her thirties. I sat on a mortar next to a little girl about six years old and began shelling corn. The woman soon went into the kitchen and began to dish out the food. She called in the little girl, who soon returned with a plate of cornmeal, greens, slices of avocado, and a spoon. She handed the plate to an elderly man and returned to the kitchen. After everyone was served, she asked me, "Do you want some?" in a sweet and innocent voice.

"Oui," I replied, feeling embarrassed. She returned to the kitchen and told her mother, who sent me a small portion without avocado in a calabash bowl.

"No more spoons," said the child.

"Merci," I replied, taking the food. I ate with my fingers and drank from a tin can near the water well. While everyone was busy eating, I slipped two corn cobs in my pocket, thanked the woman, and left. In Chelaine's kitchen, I roasted both ears on her stove of three coconut-size stones, ate, and saved the naked cobs to use as toilet paper when I went in the underbrush. Going to neighbors' houses whenever I smelled food became a habit for me.

Early Monday morning, I restuffed my shoes with scraps of fabric and put on my last set of clean clothes. The daily corn flour was not ready.

"I am going to school now," I said.

"Okay, I'll save your food," said Chelaine. I left the house, carrying my old notebooks from Port-au-Prince and a pencil. I bought two pieces of corncake from a street vendor for breakfast, using my last two pennies. As I approached the school, I noticed Maître Jean-Charles standing at the open gate with a long cowhide whip dangling from his belt like a sword. He reminded me of an overseer I had seen in a picture about slavery in Saint Domingue. Each student greeted him with "Bonjour, Maître Jean-Charles," and he answered with a simple "Bonjour."

At five minutes before eight, he rang a small hand bell as students rushed into three class-huts. I waited outside until Maître Jean-Charles escorted me into a class-hut and told the teacher, a tall man with coal-black skin, "This is Jean-Robert Cadet. He belongs in the eighth grade." In the class-hut there were two rows of desks and two students at each desk. The eighth grade sat in the row on the teacher's right. I was assigned to the sixth desk back, making me the twelfth student in the eighth grade. The other row, on the teacher's left, was for the twelve seventh-grade students.

Looking out the window, I could see the class-hut next to mine, which housed the ninth and tenth graders. Just past it was the class-hut for the juniors and seniors. Maître Jean-Charles taught the juniors and seniors. There were two girls in the school, and both were in Maître Jean-Charles' class, preparing for the national exam.

Each teacher was equipped with a cowhide whip to use on students who came in late or made mistakes at the blackboard.

An older student walked in and handed me three books. "These are from Maître Jean-Charles," he said and walked back to his class.

There was one top student at each grade level. They were sent to the board usually to correct mistakes made by others. Students rarely raised their hands. They were called upon to recite a lesson, give an answer, or go to the board. Every pupil was focused at all times.

Almajipe Bello, a tall eighth grader who was a shade darker than I, was considered the most intelligent eighth grader because of his light skin. Even the dark-skinned professor seemed to acknowledge that, because sometimes he rewarded Almajipe with a smile and the words "petit blanc," the highest praise for intelligence. That morning at least five students were whipped in front of the blackboard with the rigoise.

During the thirty-minute recess, every student in the eighth grade seemed to focus on me, asking, "Are you smart? Are you as smart as Almajipe Bello?" Almajipe was angry because he was no longer the center of attention. He walked over and stared me down. I was worried. I thought he was going to hit me.

"I am ten times smarter than you," he said. The professor looked on and smiled broadly.

At five minutes before noon, the professor wrote the math assignment on the board. "Get ready for this afternoon," he said with a dare in his voice. Almajipe turned his head toward me and smiled.

Once in the street, Almajipe yelled, "Hey, Jean-Robert. You gonna get it this afternoon."

At Chelaine's house, I ate dinner and inspected the three used books. Inside each cover was the name "Bach Jean-Charles." He was Maître Jean-Charles' son, a senior, preparing to go to Port-au-Prince to take the national examination. I did the assignments and reviewed business math problems in my old notebooks.

At half past one, I returned to school and waited for the two o'clock session to begin. Almajipe was in the yard, taunting me. "You gonna get it this afternoon," he was saying. At five minutes before two, everyone was in his seat.

It was a hot and humid day. The odor of perspiring bodies had drowned the smell of the newly filled inkwells in the students' desks. After the bell rang, the professor walked in. Everyone stood up. He motioned with his hand and everyone sat quietly. Before the professor gave instructions, the father of an eighth-grade boy walked in as if he had been expected. Everyone rose and remained standing. The professor called the boy to the front of the class and handed the father the rigoise. Without being told, the boy dropped to his knees in front of the faded blackboard, and his father struck him on the back at least twenty times. The boy let out a short and muffled "Hum" at the landing of each strike. He tried not to cry, but the tears kept on flowing. Afterward, the father thanked the professor for the use of the cowhide whip and sent his son back to his seat. "He will not do it again," said the boy's father as he walked out. The professor smiled broadly, licked his lips, and signaled the students to sit.

He began with the seventh graders while the eighth graders reviewed. Each student who made mistakes knelt in a corner at the front of the room. Before the professor worked with the eighth graders, the kneeling students hunched their backs and tucked in their necks between their shoulders until they resembled turtles. The professor whipped each child on the back. Those who dared to raise their hands were dealt with more severely.

"Jean-Robert Cadet, go to the board with your book," said the professor. My heart raced. I was instructed to do a math problem from a particular page.

After I was done, the professor asked, "Are there any errors?" The class was totally quiet. It seemed that no one was breathing. Not a hand was raised.

"Almajipe Bello, go to the board and make corrections," instructed the professor. Almajipe smiled at me as he approached the board. I handed him the chalk and stepped aside. My heart was pounding. Almajipe erased a few numbers and wrote something else. I frowned. The professor smiled. Almajipe stepped aside, handing the chalk to the professor, who corrected Almajipe and replaced the numbers that I had written.

"Get on your knees," he told Almajipe. As I returned to my seat, the professor looked at me and said "Petit blanc" with a smile. Almajipe was whipped with the rigoise.

During the afternoon recess, every student in the eighth grade taunted Almajipe, shouting that he was no longer number one. Furious, he walked toward me and said, "I'll show you after school who's number one," waving his fist. At four o'clock the bell rang. School was dismissed. News of a fight was heard by every student.

Once we were a block away from the school, everyone stopped and formed a circle around Almajipe and me. I was trembling with fear. An eighth-grade student, eager to see a fight, walked toward me and offered to hold my books. I looked into the crowd and noticed the senior who had been sent to my class by Maître Jean-Charles to give me the books. I walked toward him. "Here, hold my books," I said, hoping he would prevent the fight from taking place. The senior took the books from me with a worried look on his face.

"Hey, Almajipe! If you fight Jean-Robert, I will tell Maître Jean-Charles, and you know how he feels about vagabonds fighting in the streets," he said. Almajipe looked at the senior and thought for a moment. Then he took his books from a boy and walked out of the circle without a word. I breathed a sigh of relief. The crowd dispersed.

During eighth-grade recess, I would watch Maître Jean-Charles with his rigoise standing behind a student at the blackboard. For every mistake the student made, Maître Jean-Charles would strike him on his back as he shouted, "Crétin! Cochon marron! [Idiot! Wild pig!]" A student who arrived late to class would receive twenty lashes in the palms of his hands. As he was whipped, the student alternated hands and counted aloud the strokes through clinched teeth.

At the end of each quarter, Maître Jean-Charles called an assembly in the school yard to distribute report cards. As he called the ranking, name, and the grade point average of each student, starting with the seniors, everyone stood silently at attention. The grade point average was based on a scale of 10.0. As he reached the names of those with a grade point average below 6.0, he yelled "Crétin" at them.

In my class, I was always first, with a grade point average of 9.5 or better. Almajipe was second and Raoul Bonhomme was third. For many students, the goal was not to become educated but to avoid being savagely whipped and publicly labeled a *crétin* by Maître Jean-Charles.

The following afternoon I was sent to the board to correct Almajipe. Before I left my seat, I compared Almajipe's solution to what I had written in my notebook.

"Maître, his solution and mine are the same. There are no mistakes," I said. Almajipe smiled and I returned the smile. The professor agreed and praised me with "Petit blanc."

One hot muggy afternoon, Chelaine had no water in the house with which to cook. She and I made a trip to the Artibonite Canal with a borrowed donkey on which to carry calabashes filled with water. I lost track of time and arrived late at school. As I entered the class, the professor ordered me to kneel in a corner.

"There's no excuse for coming to class late," he said. That was my first time in the corner. Before class ended, the professor struck me on the back with the cowhide whip. I tried to protect my head by raising my hands. "How dare you raise your hands!" he said with uncontrollable rage. Each strike felt like a cigarette was being extinguished on my back. My shirt was spotted with blood but I shed no tears. That afternoon, when I arrived at Chelaine's house, she looked at me and said, "You received a beating, didn't you?" I nodded yes with my head. Before supper, I memorized the assigned pages in the textbook on Haiti's history and practiced three dictations in the French grammar text before darkness began to set in. That night seemed very long. While Chelaine and Antoine were engaging in their usual activities, my skin felt like it was on fire. The salt in my sweat caused my wounds to sting like bees.

Antoine was getting impatient with me. It had been nearly three weeks since I told him and Chelaine that I had written to my father requesting money.

"Why don't you write another letter and give it to Louis? He buys coffee for Blanc Philippe and he goes to Port-au-Prince every two weeks," said Chelaine. My eyes lit up.

"Where does he live?" I asked anxiously. After Chelaine gave me directions to Louis's house, I ran out across a neighbor's yard to the street. Running nearly two miles, I found the house. I opened the freshly painted gate and walked in. It was a much nicer place than Grannie used to have. The kitchen alone was much bigger than Chelaine's hut. The water well was cemented and covered. The oinking of pigs, the clucking of chickens, and the baaing of goats filled the backyard.

A little boy about eight years old came out of the kitchen. "Aunt Maude, someone is here," he shouted.

A brown-complexioned woman about five feet tall, wearing a new dress and sandals, came out to greet me. Before I could utter a word, she asked, "You must be Alfrenold?"

"Non, my name is Bobby," I answered, thinking I had the wrong house.

"You are the child of the late Henrilia Brutus—your mama named you Alfrenold Brutus. Your new mama must have changed your name to Bobby," she explained.

"How did you know me?" I asked, surprised.

"You look just like Blanc Philippe, and Louis told me all about your mother," she answered. I was not impressed with the name *Alfrenold*, but I wished I had been able to keep *Brutus*, my mother's family name. That way I would not have had to endure Florence's constant threat to take back the name *Cadet* and replace it with the commonplace *Joseph*.

Before long, Louis opened the gate and walked in with a new black bicycle. He was medium-built with a dark complexion and in his forties.

"Is this Alfrenold, Blanc Philippe's boy?" he asked.

Before I could answer, the woman said, "Yes, he is, but his name is Bobby now."

"Did you come with Madame Cadet?" asked Louis. Again she interrupted. "Look at him. Just look at him! He looks so much like Blanc." I was shocked and surprised, for no one had ever been so excited to see me before.

"Non, I didn't come with Madame Cadet—she went à l'étranger," I said.

"Will she send for you?" asked Louis.

"I don't know," I replied. "How did you know me?" I added.

"After Henrilia died, I carried you to Blanc Philippe and he took you to Madame Cadet. You were just learning to walk," said Louis.

"Can I live here with you?" I asked.

"Yes, this is your house. You can consider me your Aunt Maude," answered the woman. She was Louis's wife.

"I'll be back about five o'clock," I said, running back to Chelaine's house.

"Did you find him?" asked Chelaine.

"Yes, I found him and he said okay," I replied, grabbing my books to rush to school. Once in the street, I hopped and skipped all the way to school.

At four o'clock, I rushed back to Chelaine's and said nervously, "I am going to live with Louis now." Chelaine stopped sewing. She seemed stunned by the news.

"What about the money? Antoine wants his money," she said. I pulled out my box from under her bed and ran out.

When I arrived at Louis's house, Maude was waiting for me. A table was set on the back porch with porcelain plates, silverware, and drinking glasses.

"Dinner is ready. Come and eat," she said, smiling. I was so overwhelmed by her hospitality that I felt uncomfortable.

"Thank you," I said as I placed myself awkwardly at the table.

"Serve yourself. Eat as much as you want—it's all for you," she said. I was shaking with nervousness. I had never sat at a dining table to eat with other people before. Maude had three separate porcelain bowls on the table, and each one contained something different—chicken with eggplant, white rice, and red bean sauce.

"What part of the chicken do you like?" she asked.

"I don't know," I said, because no one ever asked me that question before. I felt ill at ease. Maude served me a leg and a thigh along with rice and sauce. She sat and ate with me. I felt important yet uncomfortable.

"Bobby, don't be nervous. This is your home. Consider me your Aunt Maude," she reassured me. I was speechless. I began to perspire as I enjoyed the delicious meal.

When dinner was finally over, Chelaine walked into the yard.

"Honor," she shouted, a greeting visitors used to announce their presence when entering someone's domain.

"Respect," answered Maude.

"I am here to get Bobby," said Chelaine.

"He wants to live here now, and I want him to stay," said Maude. Louis came into the yard on horseback.

"My Aunt Florence Cadet sent him to live with me, and I want him back," demanded Chelaine.

"Bobby is going to live here now. That's what he wants," said Louis, holding the gate open to signal Chelaine to get out.

"You ungrateful little boy. Look at all I've done for you. Is that the way you pay me back? I fed you and washed your clothes," shouted Chelaine as she left the yard. Louis took me into the living room for a talk. I looked around. There was a small divan, a battery-powered transistor radio, a clock on a small green table, a dinette set, two chairs, and a cabinet.

"I go to Port-au-Prince every two weeks during the coffee season to see your papa. I've been working with him, buying coffee for export, since I was a young man. He used to have a factory below the hills of Cahos. That's where he met your maman, Henrilia. That Blanc Philippe, I tell you, wouldn't leave her alone. She was his cook at the factory, you know," said Louis, smiling and shaking his head.

"What happened to my maman?" I asked.

"They poisoned her. Every woman in Cahos was after Blanc Philippe. When Henrilia had you, many women were jealous of her for having a child with a blanc. She was the prettiest woman in the factory, black as coal with pretty white teeth," said Louis.

"Do you know who killed her?" I asked.

"Non, too many women didn't want to see Henrilia's life improve. In Cahos people get along better when they have nothing. Blanc was good to Henrilia. He was giving her money. Tell me about yourself. Did Madame Cadet send you on vacation? Does Blanc know that you're here?" asked Louis, who assumed that Florence had been treating me like her own son.

"Madame Cadet went à l'étranger about a month ago, and I don't know if Blanc knows that I am here," I replied.

"When I go to Port-au-Prince, I will tell Blanc that you're with me. Whatever you need, you let me know," said Louis.

Maude walked in. "Bobby is in school, Louis. Look at his books," she said, showing the books to Louis.

"Where do you go to school?" asked Louis.

"L'Ecole Maître Jean-Charles," I answered.

"Have you paid him?" he asked.

"Non," I answered.

"How much does he charge?" asked Louis.

"Three gourdes per month," I answered. Louis opened the small cabinet and pulled out a metal box, filled with neatly stacked and dirty Haitian currency. He handed me six gourdes.

"Is there anything else you need?" he asked.

"Oui, I need three notebooks," I answered.

He gave me three more gourdes and said, "Get some pencils too."

"Come with me when you finish talking with Louis. I want to show you your room," said Maude. I followed her. She pushed aside a curtain in the doorway separating the living room from her bedroom.

"This is my bedroom," she said. In front of the bed was a table with two chairs. In the corner were two clay *cruches*, or pitchers, filled with water. At the foot of the bed stood a tall cabinet. She pulled aside another curtain to reveal a smaller room.

"This is your bed," she said, pointing to a small well-made bed with a white embroidered sheet and a pillow. I looked at the bed and thought about my bedwetting. She pointed to a mat on the floor and said, "This is for Théodore." Théodore was the little boy who had announced my presence earlier.

"Non, that's not necessary. I'll sleep on the mat," I said.

"Non, I want you to have my bed. I want to sleep on the floor," said Théodore, standing at the entrance.

"Théodore doesn't mind. He likes sleeping on the floor," she said.

"I have to study now and I have homework for tomorrow," I said. It was getting dark. Maude lit a small kerosene lamp in the living room. Louis went outside to feed the pigs. I sat at the table and began to memorize the next day's lesson.

"Why do you go to school?" asked Théodore, standing at the door.

I turned toward him and said, "I like school. Do you go to school?"

"Non, I don't go to school because I don't know how to read," answered Théodore.

When it was time for bed, Maude placed a chamber pot on the floor between the bed and the mat and said goodnight.

"Goodnight, my aunt," said Théodore and I in unison. I persuaded Théodore to take back the bed and slept on the mat, using a pillow under my head for the very first time.

Early the next morning, Théodore discovered that I had wet the mat.

"Aunt Maude, Bobby wet the mat," he said.

"That's enough, Théodore—Bobby had an accident," she replied. I was embarrassed yet I felt safe.

Maude's brother brought one of the cows from the rice field into the yard and milked it. Coffee was made; fresh bread was delivered. After breakfast, Louis told me to take the bicycle to school, but I didn't know how to ride. I taught myself, using the wall along the house to maintain my balance. After a few days, I started going to school on the bicycle. I became the envy of every student. Maître Jean-Charles would ask, "Jean-Robert Cadet, did you find the pot of gold at the end of the rainbow?"

On Saturdays I worked with Louis at the coffee depot, weighing and checking coffee beans for moisture. I also helped him verify every major transaction. Whenever I discovered an error, Louis would smile and say, "You are truly the son of a blanc."

During rice-planting seasons, Louis took me to his combites, where men with bare backs, women, and children worked all day long, sticking newly germinated rice plants into a soaked field in exchange for two meals. Yams with milk were served at noon and yellow cornmeal covered with red bean sauce at day's end, both in calabash bowls. The women led the men in voodoo songs, which seemed to help them cope with the sun's anger. Louis did not want me to plant rice because I was the son of a blanc. He thought that my light-brown skin could not tolerate the rays of an angry sun all day long.

My duty was always to fetch water from a nearby spring at the foot of a magnificent tree with thick crawling vines and the voice of a thousand cicadas. Its wide green canopy carefully shielded the sun's glaring rays, creating a cool dusky chamber below. Spanish moss dangled from the branches in every direction like unkempt hair of a lady monster in a nightmare. The spring was a perfectly cone-shaped crater, built with specks of sands as fine as brown sugar. The water was always crystal clear, sweet, and vibrating at the bottom, like a transparent hand searching for a perfect place to pin one or two floating grains of sand. With pounding heart I would press down the large calabash, drowning it in nature's cup. I kept my eyes fixed on the tree because people said that was where the *maître* of the spring—supposedly a big serpent—resided. I carried the water to the rice field and poured it in tin cups. It was so cold, the workers always drank it cautiously.

After work, everyone went to a pond near the spring to wash off. The water was usually very warm on the surface but very cold below.

Every Sunday morning, Louis took me to watch cockfights in small mountain villages. The roosters' necks and legs were shaved and toughened. Their long curvy spurs were sharpened in preparation for battle in an arena-like pit surrounded by wooden benches. The participants arrived on horseback, wearing straw hats and cradling their hooded cocks against their chests with one arm like newborn babies. From their belts hung long machetes in brown leather sheaths. Before each fight, they sprayed their fighters front and back with water from their mouths. In their shoulder bags were small bottles with garlic skins, vervain, and cinnamon bark soaking in tafia. They placed their bets in old faded and sometimes ragged Haitian currency. And during the bloody fights, they egged on their cocks with shouts of "Kill him! Get him and pierce his eyes!" Some laughed and smiled, exposing their blackened teeth delightedly. Louis had told me that most of the participants with red shirts and blue jeans were *houngans*, or witch doctors. Nearby was a large arbor covered with straw where cooked food was sold and served on plates of smoked banana leaves by women. Whenever Louis's cock won, he took the loser home for his wife to cook and left the winner with its trainer.

Returning to Louis's house from school one Monday evening, I discovered Maude's brother 'Ti' Bobo hog-tying a dog on the ground near the kitchen hut. Maude and Théodore were sitting on a large mortar and watching. The petrified dog had its tail pressed between its legs, and its ribs showed through its brown coat.

"What's going on? What are you going to do with the dog?" I asked.

"He raided the chicken coop, and I am going to teach him never to steal eggs again," answered 'Ti' Bobo with a grin. Suddenly Denis's voice echoed in my head: "I am taking you to the police station. That will teach you never to steal again." I felt a chill running down my spine and, for a brief moment, I saw myself hogtied on the ground instead of the dog.

Over a three-stone stove on the ground in the middle of the kitchen hut, a white egg was boiling. 'Ti' Bobo removed the hot boiled egg from the pot with a large wooden spoon and placed it in front of the dog's cold black nose. He then forced open the dog's mouth with a stick, shoved in the steamy egg, and held the dog's mouth shut. As the animal struggled to get free, its muffled cries and teary eyes made me tremble. After 'Ti' Bobo cut it loose, the steamy egg fell out of its mouth. The dog ran out of the yard yelping painfully.

Early one morning, the sound of a conch shell traveled through the yard. Louis rushed out of the house and noticed that one of the pigs he had been fattening was missing. He hopped on his horse with a machete and ordered me to follow him on the bicycle. As we approached a small cornfield, we heard a man shouting repeatedly, "Pig farmer, I took my share. Come get yours." Hanging from the branch of a small mango tree on the roadside near the farm was Louis's pig. The two front legs, one rear leg, and the head were missing.

Louis shook his head in disgust and said, "I bet my pig didn't even eat that much from his crop for him to kill it." Louis cut the rope, dropping the carcass to the ground. We then tied it on the back of the horse and returned home with a few dogs trailing behind. The rest of the animal was cut and sent to market.

The farmer could have held the animal for ransom, but since it was big and fat he settled for the meat instead. "If one of his animals ever gets loose and wanders into my yard, I will kill it," said Louis angrily.

11 **Late one night** I was awakened by the sound of a heavy rain beating on the tin roof. Théodore was sleeping soundly. Louis was arguing with his wife. Suddenly I heard the sound of a slap. Maude cried out. Another slap, another scream. I slowly pulled the curtain aside to observe. The small lamp was lit on the table. She was pinned down by a naked Louis. He slapped her again. She screamed louder. I jumped on Louis's back and screamed, "Leave my aunt alone." Louis dragged me back in the other room, slapped me numerous times on my rear end, and went to sleep in the living room. The next morning, Maude's face was badly swollen.

"Thank you for coming to my rescue last night," she said.

"Why was he beating you?" I asked.

"We can't have children," she responded. I was confused by her answer.

"He was beating you because you can't have children?" I asked.

"Louis is neither man nor woman," she said.

"Huh? I went swimming with him in the canal Sunday after the cockfight. I saw his penis. He is a man," I said, feeling even more confused.

"He can't do it," she said.

"He can't do what?" I asked.

"I can't explain it to you, but someday you'll understand," she said.

The following night, a man wearing a red shirt was in the living room talking with Louis and Maude. When they thought Théodore and I were asleep, they moved into the bedroom and sat at the table. Someone blew out the lamp. The darkness was thick. The man began to chant. I was listening. Théodore was sleeping soundly. Suddenly the table began to shake and bounce against the cement floor like it had a life of its own. The man's voice changed, sounding more and more like a growling bear in a cave. His words were incomprehensible. My heart was pounding. I was petrified. Suddenly I remembered the catechism I had memorized in preparation for my First Communion and I began to recite several pages, including "Our Father which art in heaven." When I ran out of prayers, I tried to recall passages I had read from Florence's prayer book when she was at the neighbor's house. I remembered "Je renonce au Satan et à ses oeuvres. Je m'attache à Jesus Christ pour toujours [I renounce Satan and his works. I will cleave to Jesus Christ forever]" and began to repeat it over and over until the séance ended. Someone lit the lamp and the stranger left. After a brief conversation, Louis blew out the lamp and all was peaceful.

Every other night for nearly two weeks the seances continued. I did not want to live with Louis anymore, and I didn't want to go back to either Chelaine or Grannie's house.

I decided to confront Maude.

"Aunt Maude, last night I heard a lot of noises. Maybe I was dreaming. Did you hear something?" I asked.

"You were not dreaming, Bobby. Did the noise frighten you?" she asked with concern.

"Yes, what was it?" I asked.

"The man who's been coming here is a friend of Louis. He's helping us find out why we can't have children," she said sadly.

"Did he tell you why you can't have children?" I asked.

"Someone had arranged a chair for Louis," she said.

"Huh? What does arranging a chair have to do with not being able to have children?" I asked.

"You can never tell anyone, Bobby—this is our secret. Someone put a bad powder in a chair for Louis and he sat on it. That's why he can't function as a man to make me pregnant. Do you understand?" she explained. I nodded yes even though I still did not fully understand.

"Do you know who did it?" I asked.

"We know who did it, and Louis is gonna take care of him," she said with teary eyes.

"Do you know why he did it?" I asked.

"For the same reason someone killed your maman. A lot of people want to do bad things to Louis because he is a well-to-do man. He has land and cows, and he buys coffee for Blanc Philippe. They don't want him to have children to inherit anything from him," she said.

Later that evening, the man who had performed the séances returned with a shoulder bag called a *macoute*, and Louis showed him into the living room. After a while, Louis called in Maude to join him and his friend. When the visitor left, I asked Maude if he was coming back.

"He's not coming back, Bobby. It's all over. He told us what to do," she said.

Théodore and I were asleep when Louis came to the room later that night and woke me up. "Hey, Bobby, wake up," said Louis, shaking me. He was holding a small kerosene lamp.

"Oui, Louis," I said, sitting up on the mat.

"Here, I want you to write the name *Edward* for me on this piece of paper," he said. Without asking any questions, I printed "Edward" on the paper and gave it back to Louis.

"Merci," said Louis and left the room.

I lay down, but before I fell asleep I heard a horse leaving the yard. The next morning I asked Maude why Louis had asked me to write the name *Edward* on a piece of paper.

"He needed the name to put in the calabash bowl," she said.

"Why? What will that do?" I asked.

"The man who was helping us sent Louis to the Artibonite River last night. He had arranged a calabash bowl for us. He told Louis to light a black wax candle in the middle of the bowl, put the name in it, and let it float down the river," she explained.

"What will happen then?" I asked anxiously.

"When the bowl sinks, Edward will die. Perhaps Louis and I will be able to have children," she said.

I felt betrayed. I was overwhelmed by guilt and I felt responsible for Edward's death.

"Why didn't he write the name himself?" I asked.

"Because Louis cannot write," she said.

Suddenly I thought about the Fifth Commandment. "Thou shalt not kill" began to echo in my mind. And I remembered Grannie Alcée's saying, "Whoever points a finger and says, 'Look, a snake!' is the one responsible for the snake's death." She had told me that saying the day she had her pig slaughtered. I had noticed a small green snake slithering near the water well and said excitedly, "Simon, look—a snake!" Simon took a machete, cut its head off, and threw the body at me. A very angry Grannie told Simon that the snake could have been a *mystère*, or a loa. Grannie shook her finger at me and said, "Whoever points a finger and says, 'Look, a snake!' is the one who kills the snake." I was petrified and thought that the *mystère* was going to retaliate against me for causing the snake's death. As far as I was concerned, writing Edward's name for Louis to put in the calabash bowl was the same as alerting Simon to the snake.

Instead of going to school I went for a long walk, heading in the direction of Port-au-Prince until hunger forced me to return to Louis's house late at night. I was angry and I refused to talk to anyone. I stopped going to the coffee depot and on Sundays I refused to go to his cockfights.

"You're not the same boy who first came to live with us," Louis would say to me, while I stared at him disgustedly.

Early one Saturday evening, I went to a concert with a neighborhood friend who was much older than I was. The moon was so bright I lost track of time. The concert took place under a huge tree in the middle of a large open field. The musicians played trumpets, drums, bamboo tubes, maracas, and cymbals. I did not return until three o'clock in the morning. After breakfast, Louis cut a long switch. He stood near the outhouse and summoned me. "Come here, little boy, I am gonna teach you a lesson," he said.

Nervously I picked up two rocks the size of mangoes. "If you touch me, I'll break your head open, and I swear it," I yelled. Louis was shocked. His mouth fell open.

Maude intervened, taking the switch from her husband. "What did he ever do to you?" she asked. Louis grabbed his bicycle and left the yard.

That night while everyone was asleep, I took the clock from the living room, set it for three in the morning, and placed it under my pillow. The pounding of my heart and the muffled ticking of the clock seemed to have joined in a conspiracy to keep me awake. Before the alarm could wake anyone up, I turned it off. I put on my shoes, grabbed my box, and slowly unhooked the door latch. I stepped outside and slowly closed the door behind me. As I opened the gate to leave the yard, I looked up, searching the dark, somber sky for loups-garous who might have been flying back home before sunrise. I prayed that I wouldn't be abducted by a band of RaRa, musicians often thought to be loups-garous. I ran all the way to the town square, where the bus God Is Great was waiting to leave for Port-au-Prince.

Breathlessly I told the driver, "Louis is sending me to Port-au-Prince on an errand, and he told me to pay you on my way back."

"Okay, get on board," said the driver. I slept on the bus and woke up in Port-au-Prince about nine o'clock that morning. I thought about going to the Villards' house but changed my mind, thinking that Yvette would never allow me to stay. I remembered Louis talking about Blanc Philippe living at 18 Rue Bernard, so I decided to go there instead. I asked strangers in the streets for directions to Rue Bernard until I found it and on it a big yellow house with the number 18.

I stood across the street, nervously observing activities in the yard. Two cars were parked in the driveway. I observed a white man getting into one, a black VW bug. I crossed the street and walked toward the car as it began to back out. The driver noticed me and stopped. He got out of the car and asked with a harsh tone, "What are you doing here?"

"I don't want to live with Louis anymore," I answered, trembling with my box in my hands.

"Where do you want to live?" asked Philippe harshly.

"I want to live here with you," I answered, my heart racing.

"You can't live with me. What am I gonna do with you? Get in the car," he snapped. I put my box in the backseat and sat in front.

"Are you hungry?" asked Philippe, backing out of the driveway.

"Oui," I answered.

There was a long silence until Philippe parked in front of a cafe. "Let's get something to eat," he said. Inside, Philippe sat on a stool at the bar and I sat nervously next to him, looking straight ahead to avoid eye contact.

"Two chicken sandwiches, two guanabana juices, and one black coffee," ordered Philippe. The server walked away. The traffic noise could not break the silence. I lifted my head and gazed at the slow-moving ceiling fan until the food was placed in front of us. I looked at Philippe from the corner of my eye, waiting for him to touch his food before I touched mine. With trembling hands, I took a small bite and began to chew in slow motion.

"Can't you eat any faster? I am in a hurry," snapped Philippe. Without looking at him, I took bigger bites and swallowed. Then I poured the juice down my throat. Philippe was still eating.

"Let's go," he said, leaving a few bites on the counter. I jumped off the stool and rushed to the car. After a few minutes of driving, he said, "I am gonna ask a friend of mine to take you in until I send you to Florence in New York." I continued to look at him from the corner of my eye until he pulled into a driveway a few blocks away from his house.

"Wait in the car," he said. He walked toward a plump, brown-complexioned woman sitting on the front porch and kissed her on both cheeks. After he talked with her for about five minutes, he waved at me to come forward.

"This is Madame Laroche. You're gonna be staying with her until I send you to New York," said Philippe, pulling out his wallet. He handed her a few dollars, kissed her good-bye, and said, "I'll see you in two weeks." I stood silently watching my father's car leaving the driveway.

"What's your name?" asked Madame Laroche.

"My name is Bobby," I answered glumly.

"Bobby who?" she asked.

"Bobby Cadet," I replied.

"Oh, your father didn't give you his name, did he, Bobby Cadet? You're an embarrassment to him, aren't you? You'll be staying here until you go to New York. Philippe is such a good man, you're very lucky," she said.

It was a two-story wood frame house with indoor plumbing. I followed her upstairs with my box and she told me to place it under a small iron bed.

"This is my son's room—you'll be sleeping here. I'll put a mattress on the floor for you. Jérôme is in school now. He'll be home at five," she said. She opened another door.

"This is Mademoiselle Marie-Claire's room. She's also in school." Finally she opened a third room. "This is my room," she said, and quickly closed the door, preventing me from taking a good look at her voodoo shrine. I followed her back downstairs and she showed me the bathroom, dining room, and living room.

Later, when her children arrived, she told them about my staying temporarily, until I went to New York. Jérôme was a tenth grade student with his mother's complexion and Marie-Claire was a senior with her father's light skin. Both were in private schools.

At bedtime I told Jérôme that sometimes I wet my bed, and he quickly told his mother, who placed a mat on the floor for me instead of the intended Spanish moss mattress.

"If you're still wetting your bed, you must be sick," said Madame Laroche.

Bored with sitting around all day with nothing to do, I asked Madame Laroche if there was a school that I could attend until I left for New York.

"School costs money and I don't think Philippe will spend money on school, since you're going to New York very soon," she said.

"When am I going to New York?" I asked.

"Philippe is making arrangements now. Knowing his reputation, you'll be going very soon," she replied.

"What about a public school? Ecole Simone Duvalier is not too far," I observed.

"Non, you cannot go," she snapped. Every day she made me dust in the living room. I helped myself to her son's books, reading and practicing my math skills.

One Friday evening, a small car pulled into the driveway. Before the driver stepped out, Madame Laroche said, "Come here quick." I followed her into the living room. "This young man is coming to visit Mademoiselle Marie-Claire. I want you to sit in here with them until he leaves," she said. The young man was her daughter's boyfriend. He was sometimes referred to as a "grimeau" because of his light skin. If his hair had been straight and his features less Negro, he would have been considered a mulatto. His family was very well off financially. Madame Laroche turned me into the protector of Mademoiselle Marie-Claire's virginity, as if the family's future as well as reputation rested upon it. She instructed me to follow them during afternoon walks, making sure that they didn't go into any house. Marie-Claire had to account for every minute she spent away from her house.

One evening the young man, whose name was Jérôme, offered me fifty cents to slip through the back door, to allow him a few minutes of privacy with Marie-Claire. I agreed and took the money. After a while, I thought that was a good way to earn money. Each time Jérôme asked for privacy, I charged him more. I was no longer a living chastity belt but a little pimp with an exclusive client. During an early evening promenade, Jérôme took Mademoiselle Marie-Claire to his house while his parents were away. I waited outside near the elaborate-looking gate. After nearly an hour, the young couple came out to continue their walk. I noticed that Jérôme seemed more cheerful than usual.

Whenever I had a chance, I would watch my father's house, standing across the street to observe people going in and out. One Sunday evening, while there were no cars in the driveway, I walked into the yard.

"Aren't you the young man I saw in the driveway talking to Monsieur Sébastien?" asked the maid.

"Oui," I said.

"Are you his son?" she asked.

"Oui," I replied.

"Let's go inside. I'll take you to see your grandmother," she said. I followed the housekeeper to a bedroom where a frail and pale elderly white lady was sitting in a rocking chair. Her hair was white as cotton. "Grandmère, this young man is your grandson," said the maid.

"Where is he?" she said, searching with her hands while her hazel eyes remained fixed.

"Hold her hand, she's blind," said the maid. I extended my hand and she held it firmly.

"Who is this? What is your name?" she asked in French in a soft yet crackling voice.

"My name is Bobby," I said in French.

"I don't remember any Bobby. My boys have children that I don't know anything about. Who's your father—Philippe, Pierre, or Robert?" she asked.

"Philippe," I answered.

"It's time for your bath now, Grandmère," said the maid.

"Okay, darling, you come to see me again, you hear?" she said.

"Oui," I answered. While her calling me "darling" made me feel welcome, I didn't feel wanted, and wanted was what I always wanted to be.

Going through the dining room, I noticed an open bottle of rum on the table and a bowl of sugar. Although I was not thirsty, I felt a strong desire to leave with something that belonged to my father. I poured some of the rum into a cup, mixed it with sugar, and drank it. Madelaine, Philippe's niece, walked in and discovered me while I was drunk. "Who is this boy in the house?" she yelled. The maid ran in. "His name is Bobby and he's Monsieur Philippe's son."

"What's he doing here? He's drunk. Where does he live?" she asked.

"I don't know where he lives. He came by himself," replied the maid. I vomited on the floor.

"Where do you live?" asked Madelaine. I pointed in the direction of Madame Laroche's house. A man helped me into a car.

"I'll drive you home. Can you give me directions?" he asked.

I nodded yes and gave him directions to Madame Laroche's house. He pulled into the driveway and helped me out of the car.

"He helped himself to some rum and got drunk," the driver told Madame Laroche.

"Okay, thank you for bringing him back. I'll take care of him," she said, as the driver was leaving.

She led me to the bathroom by the ear, forced me into the shower and turned on the water. Then she pulled me out and forced me down to my knees. She rushed upstairs, fetched a leather belt, and whipped me mercilessly.

"Your father is such a good man. How dare you go to his house and embarrass him and his family like that? You don't know how lucky you are to have a father like that. Philippe is such a saint," she said.

Late one morning when the sun was not yet angry, Philippe came to pick me up in a black VW. I put on my clean khaki shorts, blue plaid short-sleeve shirt, white socks, and my only shoes, a pair of white canvas sneakers. I sat nervously next to him and every so often looked at him from the corner of my eye. He drove to a section of the city near a huge statue of a black man blowing a conch shell. From the statue's arms and ankles hung broken shackles and chains. Philippe parked in front of a small one-story brick building with a sign that read "Voyage Chatelin." I followed him. I was surprised by the cool air as he opened the door. I had never been inside an air-conditioned building before. I thought about Florence's refrigerator when I opened the door. Inside were three beautiful mulatto demoiselles with shoulder-length black hair, sitting behind typewriters at their desks. They were well dressed and had the smooth skin that people often refer to as "peau airconditionée," meaning skin that is rarely exposed to the wrath of the sun.

Philippe signaled me to sit in a chair while he approached the counter. I sat with my knees close together, watching him speaking in French to one of the mulatto women in a low tone of voice. Then he waved me to follow him to a small room in the back. As I entered the room, I saw a dark-skinned man standing behind a camera on a tripod. On the wall behind him hung a black and white striped blazer and a black necktie. I stood in front of the camera while Philippe remained by the door. He said in Creole to the man, "He needs to have a picture for his passport," pointing at me. The man unhooked the blazer and helped me put it on. I looked down. It reached below my knees and my hands were confined inside the sleeves. The photographer removed a few safety pins from his pocket and altered the back and sides like a skilled tailor to make it fit. "Don't worry about the sleeves, they won't show in the picture," he said. Then he loosened the tie, slipped it over my head like a noose, and adjusted it around my shirt collar. He took my picture while I had a serious look on my face. That was the very first time I had my picture taken. After the photographer freed me from the blazer, Philippe motioned me to follow him.

Once outside, I noticed that the sun was getting angry. I used my hand as a visor and followed Philippe to the car. He drove to a bright yellow building and parked. Again I followed him. The doors were open and the mostly dark-skinned people inside had sweaty brows. A black ceiling fan was turning lazily. Philippe approached the tall counter. I stood three steps back to his right. He told a man in a white short-sleeve shirt in Creole that I was here to be vaccinated for a trip to New York.

"What is your name?" asked the clerk to me in French.

"My name is Jean-Robert Cadet," I answered, wishing that I had Philippe's last name.

"What is your mother's name?" he asked. Suddenly I thought about the name Henrilia Brutus. I was about to say it, but Philippe answered "Florence Cadet."

"What is your father's name?" I looked at Philippe, hoping he would at least acknowledge me by saying his own name. He looked at the clerk and said, "inconnu," meaning "unknown." The clerk glanced at Philippe and me for a few seconds as if he knew that I was standing beside my father. A sinking feeling came over me. I was dead inside. My heart felt like it had been struck down with a rock, like a ripe mango from a tree, and had fallen into a pool of mud and cow dung. The clerk handed me a card and directed me to a room for the vaccination while Philippe waited outside. Afterward I followed Philippe to the car and he drove me back to Madame Laroche's house.

Like a zombie I walked into the yard and was reminded again by Madame Laroche that Philippe was a saint and that I was lucky to have him for a father. I thought about what she said and came back to life, realizing that I was more fortunate than other restavecs whose "grown-ups" had gone à l'étranger and abandoned them in absolute poverty to the streets of Port-au-Prince.

A few weeks later, Philippe came and gave Madame Laroche a few bills in Haitian currency.

"I think the boy will be leaving for New York in a couple of weeks," said Philippe. I felt ashamed that he didn't mention me by name.

"He'll need some traveling clothes. He doesn't have much," she said.

"I am in a hurry, I'll take him shopping next week," said Philippe, leaving.

The following week, Philippe came and took me shopping. Again, throughout the trip no one spoke. I looked at him from the corner of my eye. I felt uncomfortable, knowing that I was an embarrassment to him. He parked in front of a store and I followed him inside. He purchased a white shirt, a necktie, and a pair of black shoes. At another store he purchased a medium-sized suitcase and then we went to a tailor's shop where I was measured for a blue suit. On the way back, he stopped at Voyage Chatelin and instructed me to wait in the car.

"You're leaving for New York next Saturday. Be ready to go by two o'clock in the afternoon," said Philippe as he returned.

"Oui, Monsieur," I answered.

At Madame Laroche's house, I transferred the contents of my cardboard box to the new suitcase. I walked out with the empty box to ask Madame Laroche where to throw it, but before I could open my mouth to talk, the maid asked, "Can I have that box?" I handed it to her, smiling.

Everyone was talking about New York as though it were a paradise where money could be found everywhere on the ground. The cook was going out of her way to treat me kindly.

"Don't forget me. If you find money on the ground, please send some of it to me," she said.

"He's gonna be like everyone else I know who's left Haiti. As soon as he walks under the *sablier* tree in front of the airport, he will forget all about us," said Madame Laroche.

"Maybe someone ought to cut down that tree," said a voice in the background.

When Philippe came to pick me up, he thanked Madame Laroche for having done him a great favor. I said good-bye to everyone, grabbed my suitcase, and sat in the car.

Throughout the trip to the airport, I observed Philippe from the corner of my eye. He had a serious look on his face. No one said a word. After he parked the car, I removed the suitcase from the backseat. As I followed him, I noticed the sablier tree and purposely walked under it.

Philippe presented my travel papers to the desk clerk while I stood beside him.

"Is he traveling alone?" asked the clerk.

"Oui, he is," answered Philippe. A baggage handler took my suitcase, placed it in the back of a small truck, and drove to the waiting airplane.

"He may go on board now, sir," said the clerk, returning my

documents to Philippe, who handed them to me. I lifted my head and looked into Philippe's eyes, wanting to shake his hand but afraid to make the first move.

"Well, what are you waiting for? Go, get on the plane," said Philippe, motioning me away with his hand. I walked to the airplane without looking back.

As I sat in a seat near a window, I looked through my travel documents. I read the passport, and it showed February 15, 1955, as my date of birth. The date on my airplane ticket was February 15, 1969. It didn't occur to me that it was my birthday, because I had never had one.

12 **During the flight,** I suffered from air sickness. I didn't know that airplanes were equipped with bathrooms. I looked in the magazine pouch in front of me and saw a beautiful white paper bag with a shiny metallic interior. I thought it was very valuable. I put it back. I was in a cold sweat. I felt sick. The airplane made a sudden drop, sending the contents of my stomach upward. I quickly removed all the magazines from the pouch, stuck my head inside, and vomited. The passenger next to me asked to be seated elsewhere. A very perturbed stewardess escorted me to the bathroom. After I washed my face, the same stewardess walked me to another seat and demonstrated what I should have done with the bag. That night the airplane landed at JFK International Airport. I was guided to a customs officer, who seemed surprised when he saw my old dented tin cup and plate in the suitcase. Florence and Denis were waiting at the terminal. I approached them carrying my suitcase and wearing a new blue suit, white shirt and tie, and shiny black shoes.

"How are you doing? How was the flight?" asked Denis.

"Bien, merci," I replied.

Florence handed me a coat. "Bobby, did you miss me? Here, put this on—it's cold outside," she said, smiling. I was swallowed by the coat. It was Denis's old coat.

"How's my maman?" she asked.

"She is very sick," I answered, thinking that I had not seen

Grannie for a long time. Once outside the terminal, I was amazed by the lights and the tall buildings. As I followed Denis and Florence to the car, I kept my eyes on the ground, searching for the rumored money. I found nothing, not even a red cent.

The trip to upstate New York seemed long. No one said a word. The silence was not too noticeable because I was preoccupied, watching the cars and the big trucks, which I thought were not equipped with horns because they were so silent. It was nearly eleven o'clock when the car pulled into the driveway. I removed my suitcase from the back of the station wagon and followed the two to a small two-story brick house. Denis said good night and went to his bedroom.

"Are you hungry?" asked Florence.

"Oui," I answered, following her into the kitchen. I put down my suitcase next to the table. I looked in every corner for a small step stool. There was none. She gave me a bowl of beef stew and directed me to get a spoon from a drawer.

"Merci, oui," I said, waiting to be told where to sit. Florence, sensing that I was ill at ease, asked me to sit at the table. She pulled out a chair and sat across from me. I was nervous. I couldn't eat. It was the first time Florence had ever shared a table with me.

"Don't be embarrassed—eat," she said. I put a spoonful of stew in my mouth and swallowed.

"Where are the children?" I asked, to break the silence. It was the first time I had ever asked her a question.

"They are sleeping upstairs," she replied. I opened my suitcase, pulled out my old tin cup, and filled it with water from the faucet. She was surprised to see that I still had the same old tin cup.

"You don't have to use your own cup and plate in this house and you don't need permission to open the refrigerator anymore," she said. "Also, don't address anyone in the house as 'Monsieur,' 'Madame,' or 'Mademoiselle' in the presence of guests."

"Oui," I answered.

"Listen and listen good. Madame Denis didn't want you to come to this country. She thinks that you're going to be a bad influence on her children. You have to prove her wrong. You need to help as much as possible around the house, showing her how useful you are. Try not to do anything to upset her. This is her house, and Denis will do anything she asks of him," she said.

"Oui," I said, nodding.

"Come, I'll show you the children," she said.

Florence took my tin cup and put it in the garbage container next to the sink. I followed her upstairs to a small bedroom and looked at the sleeping children. She came back downstairs.

"There is a new baby in Lise's room. His name is Denis Jr.," she said.

"Oui," I said. She took me to a small room that used to be a small front porch. The small bed took its entire length.

"This is where you're gonna sleep. Do you still wet your bed?" she asked.

"Oui," I replied, my heart pounding. For the first time in my life I had a bed. She went to the kitchen and returned with two large plastic bags. "Here, spread these over the mattress," she said. I followed her instructions.

"Bonne nuit," she said.

"Bonne nuit," I answered. It was the first time she had ever said good night to me.

Early in the morning, my bed was dry. I put on a pair of my old shorts, filled up a small bucket with water, and went outside to wash the car. The windows and windshield were white with frost. I could barely hold the wet sponge. I was shivering. The water in the bucket turned ice cold. I heard a tap on the window. It was Denis, waving me back inside.

"We're in February, Bobby, in the middle of winter. You don't have to wash the car. Wait for summer," he said.

"Oui," I said, feeling uncomfortable being inside, because in Haiti my place was always outside or in a corner of the kitchen.

"Go put on some long pants and a long-sleeved shirt. You must be freezing," he said. I went to my room and changed into my blue suit. I had no other clothes.

The children were happy to see me. They took me by the hand to their room and showed me their toys. Lise was in the kitchen making breakfast. Florence came into the children's room.

"I want you to go down to the kitchen and say bonjour to Lise.

Set the table for breakfast and make yourself useful to her. Remember, this is her house," said Florence. I went to the kitchen. The kids followed me.

"Mommy, look! Bobby is here," said Emilie in English.

"Wonderful," replied Lise without emotion.

"Bonjour, Madame Denis," I said.

"Bonjour," replied Lise flatly.

"Bobby's gonna set the table for breakfast. Let's help him," said Emilie to her little brother Marc. I set the table for five. Emilie counted the plates.

"One for Mommy, one for Daddy . . . hey, we're missing one," she said.

"I'll eat later," I said, feeling out of place.

"Put another plate on the table," said Lise. I complied.

"Emilie, go tell Daddy and Grandma breakfast is ready," said Lise.

Everybody was seated. French toast, scrambled eggs, bacon, coffee, orange juice, and milk were on the table. Lise served the children, and the adults served themselves. I felt like my arms were too heavy to lift to serve myself.

"Excuse me," I said, as I left the table. I went to the bathroom and sat on the edge of the tub until everyone finished. I then cleared the table and ate what was left while standing in front of the sink. I washed the dishes and put them away. During subsequent meals, I stayed in my room until everyone left the table. My old routine was reestablished.

Monday morning, Denis and Lise left for work. Denis worked in a bank as a loan processor and Lise worked in a nearby rubber-stamp factory. Florence worked from four to midnight at Letchworth Village, an institution for the mentally ill.

Alix, Lise's little brother who worked on the same ward as Florence, came for a visit. He brought a bag of second-hand winter clothes and handed it to me. He had known me in Haiti as a restavec.

"You have to send Bobby to school, you know. It's against the law in this country not to send a minor to school," he said.

"Could you take him for me?" asked Florence.

"Okay, but he needs his passport," said Alix.

"Bobby, get your passport. Alix is gonna take you to school," said Florence. I took my passport out of my suitcase and followed him to his car. He drove me to Kakiat Junior High School in Spring Valley, New York. I was in awe. The school was absolutely beautiful. I could see my reflection on the shiny floors. As I walked down the long hallway to the office, my eyes were fixed on the ceiling lights. The smell was totally unfamiliar to me, unlike any school I had ever been in. At the office, Alix handed my passport to a very white woman and said something in English. She seemed to type everything Alix said about me. After Alix left, two white male students came to the office and escorted me to a room where I was issued four books. Then they directed me to a classroom where a tall bearded white teacher assigned me a seat next to a freckle-faced boy with red hair. He looked so strange to me. Every student turned to look at me. I was the only black kid in the class.

"These blancs must be the most intelligent students in the entire world. How can I compete with them? They look so pale," I said to myself, thinking about my teacher at Ecole Jean-Charles. I looked in every corner of the room, searching for a whip. There was none.

"Oh my God, everyone is so smart that the teacher does not need a whip. Maybe when he realizes that everyone is smarter than I am, he will bring a whip just for me," I thought. Boys and girls were raising their hands, giving answers. The teacher seemed pleased, nodding his head in agreement. I tried to read the words on the "green board" but I could not. I had no idea which book to open and what subject was being discussed. I felt like my brain had been removed. I wanted to crawl under the desk and disappear. Finally, an unfamiliar sound signaled the end of that class. The next class was not as intimidating. It was math. This time I felt like my brain was working but my ears were not. The teacher and the students were making noises that were totally foreign to me. At one point, the teacher wrote a math problem on the board to which I knew the answer. Some students raised their hands, but I kept mine on the desk because my mouth could not make those odd sounds.

After each period, one of the boys met me outside the door and escorted me silently to the next class. Then came lunchtime. I stood in the food line like everyone else. I thought about one of my public schools in Haiti, Ecole du Canada, where students stood in line holding their tin cups to receive free diluted powdered milk for lunch. I imitated the little blanc in front of me, putting on my own tray whatever he put on his. At the head of the line, there was an overweight white lady in a white uniform sitting behind a cash register. When I reached her, she counted the items on my tray and said something that was unfamiliar to my ears. Since I had nothing in my pocket, I stood still. She made that same sound again, confusing me even more. The little blanc behind me shouted something. I turned to look at him and noticed everyone else was restless. Finally I left the tray and ran outside, to be chased back in by a freezing wind blowing powdered ice in my face. Some students laughed and pointed at me. I spent the day without lunch.

In the next class, I took comfort at seeing two black boys despite their hair, which reminded me of a black turkey primping its feathers. At the end of the class, I approached the two black boys and said "Bonjour," hoping they would understand. They looked at me with a frown and walked away.

At the end of the day, a white woman led me to a school bus, pointed at number 569, and walked away. I boarded the bus and sat next to a white girl with hair that reminded me of the tail of a white horse.

The school bus dropped me off at the corner of Johnson Street and I walked the rest of the way to Lise's house.

I found Florence, dressed in a white uniform, waiting for her ride to Letchworth Village. The children had gotten home from school. Florence handed me a plate of food. I was surprised to see that it was part of the same meal she had prepared for her family. She actually gave me a meaty piece of the chicken instead of the feet and head, which were always reserved for me in Haiti. I soon learned that in this country chickens were sold dead—without feet, heads, or feathers.

"Eat now before Lise gets home. She walks in every day at half past five and Denis comes in at six. When you're done, set the table. Stay in your room while they're eating. Wash the dishes when they are done and mop the kitchen floor. That will make Lise happy.

Remember, this is her house," said Florence as she left for work. I followed her instructions and those became the daily routine. I ate my meal standing in front of the kitchen sink.

At school the next day, an extremely beautiful white lady who taught French escorted me to her office for tutoring. She was tall with long black mermaidlike hair all the way down to her lower back. Her miniskirt and boots held my gaze. I sat beside her at a table. The fragrance of her perfume, the sight of her legs, the close proximity of her breasts to my face, and the occasional contact of our bodies, all conspired to break my concentration. Every day was the same. My body tingled and perspired. I had never felt this way before. It seemed as though I was looking at females with new eyes and my body was responding in ways that surprised me. It was a kind of harmless torture. At the sound of the bell, I walked out of her office carrying my books in front of my pants.

After nearly two months of tutoring, she sent me back to English. That day, the English teacher had a list of words on the board. I was happy to recognize most of them because of their French roots. Students were raising their hands, giving definitions. Suddenly my ears began to recognize and catch certain words.

The following morning there was a vocabulary test. As the teacher was passing out the sheets, she purposely skipped me, thinking that my English was not sufficient. Unable to verbally express my needs, I raised my hand and pointed at the test papers on her desk. She politely handed me a test. It was matching. The first word in column A was "invincible," which I had learned from Olivier's comic books. Checking the definition in column B, I noticed the word "Superman." In every definition I recognized at least one or two words. When she returned the test the next morning, I had a C. Looking at a few white students' papers, I noticed that some had D's and F's. I smiled and said to myself, "It is not true. Blancs are not smarter than I am."

At the end of the school year, I attended summer school, and then I transferred to Spring Valley High School in September.

At Spring Valley High, there were about ten Haitian students. I avoided them as much as possible, thinking that we had nothing in common besides our Caribbean accent and skin color. In Haiti I would have been their restavec, calling them Monsieur and Mademoiselle.

Mr. Rabinowitz, my history teacher, took an interest in me. That stocky white man with salt and pepper hair and the stomach of Santa Claus took me into his office every day for tutoring. He told me stories and made me read from the American history textbook. I liked the special attention, and I especially enjoyed having lunch in his office because the cafeteria was racially divided: black students who seemed angry on one side and whites on the other, with a few white teachers patrolling the center to keep the peace. I always assumed that Mr. Rabinowitz was helping me because I could not speak English, but I was wrong. He saw in my eyes a desire to learn, and he took it upon himself to give me what he thought I needed. My attitude mattered more to him than the color of my skin. He had the same goal for me that I had for myself.

In my English class, Terry—a beautiful white girl with long black hair and a round face—asked for my help with her French homework. I agreed to help her during study hall.

Her shapely plump physique made me think that her family was rich, because in Haiti plumpness suggested that a person had enough money to eat very well. And men seemed to find large women attractive.

Terry smiled at me often, making me think that she wanted to be my girlfriend. I liked her very much, but the inferior social status that I brought with me from Haiti—and my inability to communicate in English very well—prevented me from expressing my feelings.

One day she skipped study hall and took me to her house, which was near the school. Just as I had suspected, her parents were indeed very rich. The house was big and lavishly decorated. Near the fireplace in the family room was a huge and unusual-looking white piece of furniture. I pointed to it and asked what it was in broken English.

"It's a grand piano," she said smiling.

She led me to it by the hand and we both sat on the bench.

Then she took my brown fingers in her soft white hands and arranged them gently on the keys, while her long, silky, perfumed black hair brushed the side of my face like a warm tropical breeze in late afternoon. As we awkwardly played "Frère Jacques," my fingers were like snails, leaving behind trails of wetness on the ivory keys. I was certain that it was the sound of the music that kept her from hearing my heart beating against my chest.

Suddenly, a well-dressed, gray-haired woman appeared before us. "Oh hi, Grandma," said Terry. There was silence. The expression on the woman's face seemed to indicate that I was a restavec despite my clean shirt, pants, and shoes. She called Terry into the kitchen in a harsh tone of voice. After a few minutes, Terry returned to the family room looking disturbed. She asked me to leave. My feelings were not hurt because I had learned to accept an inferior status in life.

Although Terry never spoke to me again, she managed to smile at me whenever our eyes met in the hallways. I spent many days wondering how her grandmother had found out that I was a restavec. Over the next few months, I discovered that it was not my inferior social status that offended her; it was the African blood that runs through my veins and darkens my skin.

Lise's attitude toward me gradually worsened despite my usefulness around the house. American society, it seemed, was not compatible with the Haitian custom of treating children as restavecs, or slaves. She always seemed uncomfortable explaining who I was to visitors. The family members' close proximity forced by the cold weather, coupled with the social status that I brought with me from Haiti, caused tensions to flare. When I was a sophomore, she insisted that I contribute ten dollars per week for food. "You eat like a pig and you're not working," said Denis. I found a part-time job with a cleaning crew after school from 6:00 to 10:00 P.M. Monday through Friday. I walked about two miles to the Orange County Electric Company to clean offices, mopping and waxing floors. Although I met her demand of ten dollars a week, she was still not satisfied.

"From now on, I don't want you to wash your clothes in my

washing machine. You have a job, you can use the laundromat,"
she said. When the children went to bed, she wheeled the television into her room to prevent me from watching it.

After dinner, Denis left for his mistress's house, a light-skinned
Haitian woman who was his mother's best friend. At 10:00 P.M.,
when I returned from work, I'd mop the kitchen floor, set the table
for breakfast, and afterward study before going to bed. Every
morning I took the bus and ate a bagel with cream cheese at school
for breakfast. The less Lise saw me, the less irritable she was.

A few months later, I found a new job at Shopper's Paradise,
collecting shopping carts in the parking lot. I worked from 6:00
to 10:00 P.M. Monday through Friday, and from 10:00 A.M. to
6:00 P.M. on Saturdays. Every Sunday after my chores were done, I
went to the laundromat to wash my clothes and to study.

Early one Saturday afternoon, the produce manager, a middle-
aged white man, told me, "Get in the car. We have to get something from the warehouse." I got in and he drove off.

"What are we going to get?" I asked.

"I've been watching you work. You work hard. I am gonna recommend a raise for you," he said.

"Thank you, sir," I said, feeling proud of myself. He drove to a
wooded area near a park and stopped.

"I like you a lot. I want you to be my best friend," he said, placing his hand on my leg. Suddenly I thought about Simon and realized what the manager had in mind. As he moved his hand to my
crotch, I screamed, opened the door, and ran all the way to Lise's
house. Denis and Lise were surprised to see me.

"What are you doing here so early?" asked Denis. I explained
the incident.

"You left your job for that? You better go back to work; you can't
afford to lose that job," he said. When I returned to work, I saw another boy working in my place, so I went to the office.

"Did you hire a new cart boy?" I asked the secretary.

"Yes, you're fired! You can pick up your check Friday," she said. I
returned to Lise's house and told Denis that another boy was hired.

"You better find yourself another job and fast," he said angrily.

13 **When I was a junior,** a new Haitian family had just moved into a house at the end of the block. I met their son Nicolas at school. He invited me to his house to hang around and talk. I accepted his invitation because he reminded me of a poor Haitian boy. His skin was very dark and that seemed to cause his shyness when he was in the company of whites.

One Sunday evening I went to visit him as an excuse to get out of the house. There was a birthday party for his little sister. Several adults were sitting outside sipping the homemade coconut liqueur *crémasse*. Nicolas poured me a small cup. By nine o'clock, Mr. La-Fontaine, Nicolas's father, asked a friend to walk me home. The man rang the doorbell at Lise's house and waited. Lise opened the door.

"This young man had a small glass of crémasse at Mr. La-Fontaine's house. I think it went to his head," he said.

"Okay, thank you," said Lise politely. I walked in and the man left.

"Who was it, honey?" asked Denis.

"Denis, hurry, call the police. We're not going to take this anymore," shouted Lise. Denis hurried downstairs.

"What's going on?" he asked.

"Bobby's drunk. He may be on drugs. Hurry, call the police," she said. Denis went to the telephone and dialed the police. I sat on the steps with a pounding headache. Within five minutes, two white officers arrived.

"You called the police. What is the problem?" said an officer.

"This boy is drunk, and I also think he's on drugs. I want him arrested and sent back to Haiti," said Lise.

"Where does he live?" asked the same officer.

"He lives here," answered Denis. The other officer shined a flashlight in my eyes and checked my arms for needle marks.

"Are you his guardian?" asked the officer.

"In a way we are, but he's not related to us in any way. His father, who happened to be a friend of my mother's, sent him to live with us," said Denis.

"Where is your mother?" asked the officer.

"She's at work right now," replied Denis.

"I don't think he's on drugs. He may have had something to drink. What did you drink, son?" asked the officer.

"A little bit of liqueur," I answered, shaking with fear, thinking that the officers were about to take me to the police station to beat me the way the police in Haiti beat restavecs. The officer took Mr. LaFontaine's address from me.

"We'll go there and check it out. We're not Immigration. There's nothing we can do about sending him back to Haiti. Good night," said the officer.

"Get out of my face. I'll deal with you in the morning," said Denis. I went to my room and lay down, feeling like I didn't belong in the house or anywhere else.

Later that night when Florence returned from work, I heard Denis telling her how upset Lise was when I walked in drunk.

"Lise and I cannot tolerate that kind of behavior. He not only quit his job, he's drinking. Maybe he's on drugs. We might as well send him back to Haiti. I told you before that I didn't think bringing him here was a good idea," said Denis.

"Don't be upset. Please tell Lise how sorry I am that she had to witness that kind of behavior. I'll go talk to him," said Florence.

"I don't think talking will do any good. Good night, Maman," said Denis. Florence opened the door to my room and turned on the light. I sat up, shaking with fear.

"How dare you embarrass me like that? Don't you understand that this is not my house? It's Lise's house. When your father called to tell me how you showed up at his house and how embarrassed he was, I promised him that I would take you back again. I had to beg Denis and Lise to let you come and stay in their house, thinking you would be very helpful to them. You had to get drunk, and now they think you should go back to Haiti. You better get another job fast and show your appreciation to Lise for letting you stay in her house," said Florence and walked out.

At school the next morning I ran into Nicolas.

"Hey, Bobby, the police came to my house last night asking questions about what you drank. My father was mad. Why did your parents call the police?" asked Nicolas.

"They're not my parents. They are people that I am staying with," I said.

"What do you mean by 'staying with'?" asked Nicolas.

"They are friends of my father's. He sent me to live with them," I said, trying not to reveal that I was their restavec.

"Oh, now I understand," said Nicolas.

"Do you know where I can find a part-time job?" I asked.

"I know of a diner. It stays open all the time. I know someone who works there. He said that they're always hiring," said Nicolas.

"Where is it?" I asked.

Nicolas gave me directions. Later that evening, after I finished my chores, I took a bus to the diner and asked for an application.

"I need a dishwasher from ten o'clock at night to seven in the morning. If you want it, I'll give you an application," said the boss.

"I want it," I said.

"Can you start tonight?" asked the boss.

"Yes, I can," I replied.

"It's very simple. You wash dishes, you clear tables. When things are slow, you peel potatoes. You also get to eat all you want," said the boss.

"I'll be back at ten," I said, taking the bus back to Lise's house. I told Denis about the job.

"It's from 10:00 P.M. to 7:00 A.M.," I said.

"What about school? Are you quitting?" asked Denis.

"Non, school starts at eight and there is a bus that leaves from the diner and stops a block away from school," I explained.

"Okay, I'll tell Maman tomorrow morning that you're working again," said Denis.

I took my book bag and left for work. At the diner, I was given an oversized uniform and a plastic apron. I studied for an hour before starting to work. At two in the morning, when there were no customers, the boss let me sleep in a booth for an hour. Then the big trucks started pulling into the parking lot. I cleared tables and washed dishes until seven. I ate breakfast and took a bus that dropped me off a couple of blocks from school.

As I was about to go to work one evening, Denis stopped me for a talk. "Teachers have been calling, saying that you're sleeping in class. You're not learning anything; why don't you quit school and try to get a job at American Tack Company? They are always hiring," said Denis.

"Oui, I'll do that," I answered as I left for work. At the diner I told the boss to find someone else because I was quitting after that shift.

While at school, I was called into the counselor's office. I was told that my IQ score had shown that I had low intelligence. I was being placed in a class for the educable mentally retarded. The counselor suggested that I take auto body repair or welding instead of academic subjects. I refused to comply and promised to do better.

One day, the math teacher, who happened to be walking by the EMR class, noticed me and walked in.

"What are you doing here?" he asked.

"The counselor assigned me to this class," I replied.

The two teachers went into the hallway to talk. After a while, the math teacher took me to the counselor's office.

"Why did you put him in the EMR class?" he asked.

"According to his IQ scores, that's where he belongs," replied the counselor.

"Was the test given to him in French or in English?" he asked.

"In English, of course. We don't have them in French," replied the counselor.

"Did you know that he's been in this country for less than two years?" asked the math teacher. The following day, I was given a regular schedule again.

I filled out an application at American Tack Company and indicated that I was eighteen years old. I was hoping to get the three to midnight shift. The secretary told me that I would be called when something became available. In the meantime, I had enough to give Lise money for one month of room and board.

"Did you put an application in at American Tack?" asked Denis.

"Yes, they said that when something becomes available they will call me," I replied. Denis left the house.

Later that night, Lise put the children to bed and stayed in her room. I was doing my homework at the kitchen table. A few minutes later, the children came downstairs, playing and running around the table.

"Hey, stop it. Go back upstairs—you're shaking the table," I said firmly. Suddenly Lise came back down, looking disturbed.

"How dare you? Who do you think you are, talking to my children in that tone of voice? It's their house and their table. You should not be talking to my children like that. I want you out of my house right now," screamed Lise. I was stunned. I quietly went to my room, packed my suitcase and went to Nicolas's house. I knocked softly on Nicolas's window.

"Nicolas, open up. It's me—Bobby." Nicolas opened the window.

"What's the matter?" he asked.

"Lise threw me out," I said.

"What did you do?" he asked.

"I raised my voice at the children," I answered. I climbed through the window and spent the night on the floor in Nicolas's room. In the morning, Mrs. LaFontaine thought that I had come to pick up Nicolas. Every day after school I went to Nicolas's house for dinner. I ate with him either at a small table in the kitchen or in his room. The family assumed that I was visiting. After dinner, I would go to the laundromat to study until eleven o'clock and then return to Nicolas's room through the window. Whenever I heard someone coming into the room, I rolled under Nicolas's bed.

Late one night I was taking a bath. On my way out, I came face to face with Mr. LaFontaine.

"What are you doing here? Don't you have a home?" he asked.

"They threw me out," I said.

"Well, you can't live here," he said.

"I'll get my things," I said, thinking about going to the laundromat to spend the night.

"You don't have to go right now. Find somewhere else tomorrow," he said.

In the morning, I heard the family discussing my situation, and Mr. LaFontaine decided that I had to go. Since he had two teenage daughters, he was not about to let me sleep in his house.

At school, Mr. Rabinowitz approached me in the cafeteria. Ever since I had started to work at the diner, I had stopped going to his office during lunch for extra help in social studies.

"Why did you stop coming to my office?" he asked.

"The smell of your cigar is too strong for me," I replied.

"Well, I've been meaning to quit anyway. I'll make a deal with you: You come back and I'll quit smoking," said Mr. Rabinowitz with his hand on my shoulder. As we walked toward his office, tears blurred my vision and I began to sob.

"Hey, you're crying! What's wrong?" asked Mr. Rabinowitz with concern.

"I don't have anywhere to live anymore. They threw me out," I said.

"Who threw you out? What did you do?" he asked. I explained to Mr. Rabinowitz that I had raised my voice at Lise's children and she told me to get out. I was too ashamed to tell him that, as a restavec, I was not allowed to raise my voice at the children.

"When did this happen?" asked Mr. Rabinowitz.

"About a week ago," I replied.

"Was that all you did?" he asked in disbelief.

"Yes sir," I replied.

"You want me to call Lise and ask her to take you back?" he asked.

"No! Don't call! I don't want to go back," I replied.

"Why not?" asked Mr. Rabinowitz.

"I am afraid of her. Every time she cooks eggs, she places the shells on the steps in the back of the house while mumbling something. I think it's voodoo," I said. I was so afraid of Lise's ceremonies that I had purchased a small cross and wore it around my neck. I thought about the Dracula movie where a cross was used to chase away a vampire.

"Tomorrow is Thanksgiving. I'll figure out something over the holidays," said Mr. Rabinowitz.

"Denis wants me to quit school to work at American Tack, the nail factory," I said.

"Whatever you do, don't quit school. I'll see what I can do for you Monday morning," he reassured me. After school that day, I returned to Nicolas's house. Mr. LaFontaine telephoned Eddi, a bachelor friend of his who was living in a small apartment. When Eddi arrived, Mr. LaFontaine introduced me to him. He was Haitian.

"This young man needs a place to stay. He was thrown out by his folks," he said.

"I'll share my apartment with him for seventy-five dollars a month," said Eddi.

"Can you come up with the money?" asked Mr. LaFontaine.

"Yes, I'll get a job," I said. Eddi drove me to where he lived and showed me a small windowless room in an old two-story building on Main Street. The owner of the building ran an Army-Navy store on the first floor. That same day, I was hired part-time at the local A&P grocery store. My wages were barely enough for the rent. I figured on working twelve hours on Saturdays to earn extra for food.

I befriended a black American boy in the neighborhood. I went to his house around dinnertime and his mother served me a plate of food. I thanked her and she replied, "Anytime." I smiled broadly, thinking that she was going to feed me every day. After my third visit, she and her son began to see me as an intruder. On my fourth visit, they didn't let me into the house.

Monday morning, I was called into the counselor's office. Mr. Rabinowitz was waiting for me.

"Where are you living now?" asked the counselor. I told her about my arrangement with Eddi and the part-time job after school. The counselor handed me a document and directions to an address in New City, New York. I assumed that she was sending me to a better job.

"Someone at the office will be expecting you tomorrow morning," she said.

The next morning, I took a bus to New City, New York, that dropped me off in front of a small building. I walked in and was shocked to see so many people in dirty clothes waiting in line to be seen. I thought they were there to get jobs. I presented the document to the receptionist, who immediately directed me to a small booth. She read the letter to herself.

"Are you working?" she asked.

"Yes, me working part-time in A&P store in Spring Valley," I replied in broken English.

"If you quit your part-time job, you'll be eligible for full benefits," said the clerk.

"What is full benefits?" I asked.

"You'll get the full amount, food stamps, and free medical care," she explained.

"What is food stamps?" I asked, feeling confused.

"This is the Welfare Office. We will give you money to pay your rent and coupons that you can exchange for food at the grocery store. You have to quit your job at the A&P," she explained slowly.

"You give me money if me no work?" I asked, feeling even more confused.

"Yes, that is correct" she answered.

"Okay, me no go to work, you give me money," I said. I had no idea there were offices in this country where people were handed money for doing absolutely nothing. "This is even better than finding money in the streets," I said to myself, thinking about the maid at Madame Laroche's house in Port-au-Prince, Haiti, who thought that New York was some kind of paradise where money could be found anywhere on the ground.

After the paperwork was completed, I was given a check and told to report back at the end of the month for food stamps. With the food stamps, I bought TV dinners, hot dogs, and canned goods. I always felt uncomfortable paying with food stamps while other customers paid with cash.

I was soon bored with too much free time on my hands. After school I would take long walks and sit in the park. When the next check came in the mail, I was overcome with shame, knowing that my roommate was working for his pay and I was not working for mine. Reluctantly I cashed the check, paid my rent, and immediately applied for a job in an Esso station.

During the interview, the manager asked me if I knew how to make change, and I answered, "Yes sir."

"Some Esso employees have discount cards and they get 10 percent off on gas. If someone bought gas for $7.50 and handed you a discount card and a ten dollar bill, how much would you give him back?" asked the manager.

"I'd give him $2.50 plus 75 cents. That makes $3.25," I answered.

The manager smiled and said, "You're hired."

I worked from 6:00 to 11:00 P.M., Monday through Friday, and twelve hours on Saturdays. I learned as much as I could from the mechanics at the garage. On Saturdays I installed mufflers and shocks for higher pay.

One late evening, the two other gas attendants were in the locker room while I was mopping the floor.

"Hey, Bobby, come here," called the night shift manager, a college student. I leaned the mop against the wall and went into the back room. He was sitting on a bench with a small cigar box in front of him. His forearm was tied with a piece of rubber, which he held by one end in his teeth. In his free hand was a syringe, ready to be injected into his tied arm. The other attendant was sniffing a white powder nearby.

"What are you guys doing?" I asked.

"Come here and push it in my arm for me," said the shift manager.

"Hey, Bobby, you want a hit?" said the other attendant.

"I don't want a hit, and I am not gonna help you," I said and walked out. As I continued with my mopping, the general manager walked in.

"Where are the others?" he asked.

"They're in the back," I answered.

The general manager went into the locker room, fired the two attendants, and finished the shift with me. After he turned off the pumps at eleven o'clock, he said to me, "Starting tomorrow night, you're the new night shift manager. I found them doing drugs in the back. Arthur had a needle stuck in his arm." I was so excited about the promotion, I told the story to my English teacher the next morning, who told me to write it as an assignment.

Before leaving for school each morning, I usually saw my roommate, Eddi. One Monday morning he asked me about a date I had the night before.

"What did you do on your date?" asked Eddi.

"We went to a restaurant and then to the movies," I answered.

"What did you do after that?" asked Eddi.

"I took her home, and here I am," I replied.

"Did you spend money on her?" asked Eddi.

"Yes, I paid for dinner and the movie," I answered.

"Did you do it?" asked Eddi.

"No, we only kissed," I said.

"She took you for a fool, and she'll never respect you. When a woman lets you spend money on her, it means that she wants to have sex with you. A lot of times she's not going to offer anything because she doesn't want to appear easy. If you try to be a nice guy and ask, she'll say no. But their no's mean yes, especially after you spend money on them," explained Eddi.

I felt ashamed and decided not to date her again. In desperation for attention, I purposely crashed my car against a telephone pole one snowy night after work. I was not seriously hurt. The paramedic secured my neck before taking me to a hospital. I told the police to telephone Denis Cadet, hoping that someone in my former owner's family would come to see me. Somehow I had missed them because they were the only family I had ever known.

"What kind of parents do you have, kid?" asked the officer.

"Are they coming to see me?" I asked, feeling ashamed.

"They said that they were already in bed and they have to work in the morning," said the officer. Then I called Eddi. He was not home. The next day I took a taxi to the apartment.

14 **It was June of 1972.** The day of graduation was approaching. Students were signing yearbooks and telling each other of their plans for the future. The gas station was my home and the mechanics treated me like a little brother. On graduation day, I was scheduled to work the three to eleven shift.

"My class is graduating today," I told the manager.

"Well, congratulations. You don't want to miss your graduation. Go get your diploma and come back to work," he said. I rushed to school and wore my graduation gown over my work uniform. I was overwhelmed by the number of parents who came to take pictures of their sons and daughters. As the band played, I fought back tears. After my name was called, I walked on the stage, received my diploma, and went back to work.

While my Haitian peers also graduated and went on to college to become doctors, engineers, lawyers, and business men and women, some of my black American peers had dropped out of high school to become whatever high school dropouts became. As for me, I had no plans for the future. As far as I was concerned, working in the gas station was much better than being a shoeshine boy anywhere.

Walking down Main Street the following day, I noticed a big poster of a soldier driving a tank posted against the glass window of an office. The sign outside said U.S. Army Recruiting Station. I walked in.

"What can I do for you?" asked a sergeant.

"I'd like to drive that tank," I replied, pointing at the poster.

"I can arrange that," said the sergeant, shaking my hand. "My name is Staff Sergeant Johnson."

"My name is Bobby Cadet."

"Do you have a high school diploma?" asked the sergeant.

"Yes, I graduated yesterday," I answered proudly. Sergeant Johnson showed me a short film of soldiers in training which impressed me tremendously.

"Are you ready to start the process?" asked the sergeant.

"Yes, I am ready," I answered. He asked me a series of questions. "Have you ever been convicted of a crime?" "Are you addicted to drugs?" "Are you a homosexual?" "Do you have any type of police record?"

After I answered no to all his questions, he pulled out a medical form from his desk. After several more questions, to which I answered no, he asked, "Do you have a bedwetting problem?"

My heart nearly stopped. I hesitated for a second. "No," I answered.

"We're gonna do a background check. If everything's okay, we'll give you a written test. If you pass, we'll give you a physical and then we'll take you in the army," he explained. In about two weeks, the recruiter drove me to New York City for the written test. The room was crowded with about fifty recruits. I was biting my fingernails. Three sharply dressed soldiers were administering the test. One distributed pencils, while the other two issued test booklets and answer sheets.

"Do not open your test booklet until you are told to do so," said one of the soldiers. My heart was pounding.

"Open your booklets and begin," instructed a soldier. After nearly two hours, another voice said, "Stop." After the materials were collected, the prospective recruits were led across the street to a cafeteria, where lunch was served to them. After lunch, the young men returned to the test site.

"If your name is called, move to your right and through the exit. That means you did not pass," said a sergeant. When he finished calling names, the room was about half-empty. I was still in my seat, smiling.

The men were guided to another room for their physical. By midafternoon everyone was sworn in. I was officially in the United States Army, and proud. My destination was Fort Dix, New Jersey, for basic training.

In the barracks, as soon as the lights were off I pulled out my air mattress from my locker and slept on the floor to avoid the possibility of wetting my bed. Every morning each recruit had to stand in front of his locker to be inspected by the drill sergeant. The beds were always checked to make sure that the blankets were snug.

Every evening after mail call, the guys returned to the barracks, reading out loud letters from moms, dads, and girlfriends and sharing boxes full of goodies from home. I became overwhelmingly depressed. I felt empty inside.

"Hey, Cadet, smell this letter from my girl," said a bunkmate, waving a perfumed note in my face.

"Hey, Cadet, listen to this," said another.

"That's nice, that's good," I said with a fake smile.

"Hey, Cadet, don't you get letters from home, man?" asked the soldier next to me.

"I get letters," I answered abruptly, while thinking about shooting myself in the head.

One evening, while the guys were writing letters to their families and friends, I decided to write a love letter. I addressed it to myself and wrote the name Josephine Benson as the sender. At the next mail call, my name was called. Everyone seemed to notice that I had a letter. Returning to the barracks, my depression was less acute as I read it to my buddies. I continued writing nearly every evening, fabricating a mother and two more girlfriends.

During close combat training, every time I plunged my bayonet deep inside the rubber target, Florence's face flashed into my mind. And at the firing range, it seemed that Florence fell every time I hit the silhouette. Sometimes it was Lise and other times it was Denis.

After eight weeks of basic training, I was given a week off prior to reporting to South Carolina for AIT, Advanced Infantry Training. I took a bus to New York to visit Eddi. He was not at the apartment. I took another bus to the city to visit Eddi's aunt, a kind-hearted woman with a husband and two children. She told me that Eddi had gone to Canada for the weekend and invited me to stay until I reported to Fort Jackson, South Carolina. At bedtime, she placed a mattress covered with white sheets on the living room floor for me. At about three in the morning, I dreamed that I was urinating against a tree, the same dream I always had as a boy restavec in Haiti. I was awakened by a soaked mattress and sheets. When I turned on the light, I saw a trail of urine inching its way to the couch. Unable to face Eddi's aunt in the morning, I got dressed, gathered my duffel bag, and left the apartment. I took a taxi to the airport and caught a flight to South Carolina.

Arriving at my unit, I presented my military orders to the sergeant in charge, who read them with a frown.

"You're six days early, soldier. What's wrong with you? Don't you have a home or a family to be with?" he asked.

"I wanted to come early, sergeant," I said, smiling.

"Are you a Gomer Pyle?" asked the sergeant angrily.

"No, sergeant!" I answered.

"You better not be. We don't want any goddamn Gomers in this unit. Do you understand me, soldier?" yelled the sergeant.

"Yes, sergeant," I answered and followed him to an empty barracks.

"Get yourself a bunk and go to Supply for sheets and blankets.

The mess hall is behind us. Chow is at 0600, 1200, and 1700. Tomorrow morning at 0900 report to the supply sergeant, you goddamn Gomer Pyle."

That night I placed my poncho over my mattress and went to sleep. I didn't wet my bed. After breakfast, I policed the area, picking up cigarette butts as I had done in basic training. At 0900 hours, I reported to the supply sergeant.

"Good morning, Sarge," I said.

"Sur-prise! Sur-prise! So, you must be Gomer!" said the supply sergeant with a big grin on his face.

"So, Gomer, you're gonna do inventory this morning. Count every piece of equipment and write it down on this form," he said.

When AIT began, I went back to writing letters to myself to fight my depression in the barracks. When asked why I was sleeping on the floor I always replied, "I passed inspection this morning and I don't want to mess up my bunk."

I soon discovered a general lack of respect for women on the part of many enlisted men. Almost everyone I knew referred to women as "bitches." A soldier showing the picture of his girlfriend or fiancée to his buddies would brag, "Look at this bitch. Ain't she fine?" And while marching and singing cadence in the streets, the platoon sergeants or squad leaders would switch to sexually explicit songs when women were walking by.

On graduation day everyone who had successfully completed all parts of his training was given his orders. The company commander came to the barracks. Everyone stood at attention. He called me and a few guys to step forward and follow him to an office. Everyone panicked.

"The army needs volunteers for airborne training, and I like you guys. It means opportunity for promotions, and you'll get $55 a month extra for jumping out of perfectly good airplanes," he said. The guys looked at each other.

"Okay, I'll go," I said. The others also volunteered.

The graduation ceremony took place on a wide-open field. The bleachers were filled with civilians and military personnel. The band blasted the breezy air with patriotic tunes while the graduates paraded proudly in their khaki uniforms. A large stars and stripes and several unit flags of blue, red, and green floated in the cool breeze behind a large podium. The units were called to attention.

My commander stood in front of his troops. "In every graduating class, there's always an individual that stands out as the most outstanding in his unit," he said. "The officers and NCOs have selected Pfc Private First Class Jean-Robert Cadet as the best sentinel in this unit." Then he read a letter and said, "This letter will be placed in your personnel file and a copy will be sent to your parents." I felt proud. As I fought back tears, goose bumps covered my skin.

After graduation I received my orders to report for parachute training at Fort Benning, Georgia. Once again I reported early and was received with a similar frown by a sergeant who also referred to me as Gomer Pyle.

Airborne training was demanding. The troops ran everywhere they went and exercised three times a day. Some soldiers dropped out and others were given a chance to quit. Those who suffered from motion sickness, like myself, were given Dramamine.

The time came for the first jump. Everyone was sitting on the floor of an empty C-130 aircraft, wearing two parachutes, one on the back and a miniature in front. The jumpmaster walked in.

"If anyone wants to quit, now is the time. Once we're in the air, everyone must jump. Anyone who changes his mind will be thrown out. Are you ready?" he shouted.

"Yes, jumpmaster!" shouted the recruits. The plane took off and was soon in the air. My heart was pounding. I was at the head of the line and the first one to jump.

"Jumpmaster, get ready," said the pilot over the radio.

"On your feet," shouted the jumpmaster at the troops. Everyone stood up, holding the metal hook of the rip cord.

"Hook up," commanded the jumpmaster. The troops hooked up the metal end of their parachute rip cords to what looked like a clothesline running from the front to the rear of the aircraft. The jumpmaster slid the door open. A powerful gush of cold wind stormed the airplane, making it difficult to hear the jumpmaster's commands. A red light near the door came on. Everyone checked each other's parachute, making sure that everything was secured.

"Stand in the door," yelled the jumpmaster. I approached the open door and looked straight ahead at the slow-moving clouds directly in front of me. I placed the palms of my hands on the outside of the aircraft, my feet at the threshold. The red light changed to green. My stomach growled and I broke into a cold sweat.

"Go!" shouted the jumpmaster. I froze. I looked over my shoulder and saw the glass-shined boot of the jumpmaster making contact with my rear end. Suddenly my hands moved from the skin of the aircraft. I was falling upside down. As I tried to count "one thousand one, one thousand two . . ." wind rushed into my mouth and forced the words back into my throat. My parachute opened, jerking me violently upward, causing me to vomit while hanging two thousand feet in the air. After a short while, I landed hard on the ground as a strong breeze engulfed my canopy, dragging me a few feet in the tall brown grass.

I stood up, dazed and disoriented. Saliva was dripping from my lower lip. The jumpmaster rushed over and towered over me.

"Why the hell did you freeze? Do you wanna quit, soldier? Do you wanna go to a goddamn leg unit?" screamed the jumpmaster at the top of his lungs.

I looked him straight in the eye, "No, jumpmaster, I am not a quitter," I replied.

After three more jumps, I received my wings and orders to join the 82nd Airborne Division at Fort Bragg, North Carolina. I wasted no time in joining my unit, Company C, 1st Battalion, 325th Infantry. That was my new home: a combat-ready unit constantly on the move practicing combat drills.

During the first formation, the first sergeant explained rules and consequences. The two most important rules were don't go absent without leave (AWOL) and always follow the chain of command. Then the company commander introduced himself and reemphasized the former.

"Whatever problems you may have, we will help you solve them. But don't go AWOL under any circumstances," he said and walked back to his office.

"Wake-up call is at 0500, PT at 0530, chow at 0700," said the first sergeant and dismissed the troops.

In the barracks, the troops voluntarily segregated themselves. The blacks occupied one side of the bay, calling each other "nigga" and listening to Marvin Gaye and James Brown music. The whites occupied the other side, calling each other by their last names and listening to country and rock. The few Hispanics occupied the middle and played dominos. All the groups had one thing in common: They all smoked marijuana and covered its odor by burning incense sticks.

I was given a bunk on the black side of the bay. It was a hot and muggy day. I took off my shirt and sat on my bunk across from Private Williams, who was holding a roach with a pair of tweezers. He puckered and sucked in a puff.

"Hey, what's your name, nigga?" he asked.

"My name is Bobby Cadet," I answered.

"You talk funny, brotha. Where the fuck you from?" he asked, sucking another hit. He nearly burnt his lips.

"I am from Haiti," I replied.

"Where the fuck is that?" he asked frowning.

"It is a small country in the Caribbean," I replied.

"Why the fuck you talk like that, man? You talk white and sound funny," he said.

"That is the way I speak. I have an accent," I said. Private Williams opened his locker, rolled another joint, lit it, and took a long drag. He slowly blew out the smoke, making it curl back into his nostrils, and handed the joint to me.

"No thank you, I don't smoke," I said.

"What kind a nigga are you, man?" he said. I felt out of place.

"I am sorry but I don't like marijuana," I replied, looking at the strings of smoke rising slowly from a burning incense stick in an ashtray on his own footlocker.

"Fall out for formation," shouted the squad leader. Everyone quickly put on his shirt and rushed outside.

"Company ATTEN-HUT!" commanded the first sergeant. The troops snapped to attention. The company commander came out of the building.

"All present and accounted for, sir," said the first sergeant.

"At ease, men," ordered the company commander. The troops relaxed. "Tomorrow we're going on a twenty-mile hike with full combat gear. Wake-up call is at 0400 hours," announced the company commander.

"TEN-HUT!" yelled the first sergeant. The troops snapped back to attention and the company commander went back inside.

"Fall out," yelled the first sergeant. The troops went to chow. Early that evening, each group was engaging in its usual activities—smoking pot, listening to music, and playing dominos. I was sitting in my bunk, spit-shining my boots and polishing my airborne wings and sharpshooter's medal.

At 2100 hours, the lights went off and everyone went to bed. I fell asleep watching the moon through the curtainless glass windows. Private Williams lit a joint, knelt down in front of my face, and blew smoke in my nose. I woke up coughing uncontrollably. Private Williams laughed and jumped back into his bunk.

"You don't wanna smoke, I'll make you smoke, nigga," he said. I pushed my bunk near the white side of the bay and went back to sleep. At 0400 hours, the platoon sergeant turned on the lights.

"Geeet-up and get your nasty asses cleaned up," he yelled. Everyone got up, made his bed, and washed. After breakfast the troops lined up in front of the arms room with their weapons cards. I was issued an M-16 with a mounted grenade launcher. Before the hike, I marched into the platoon sergeant's office.

"Sarge, Private Williams blew marijuana smoke in my nose last night while I was sleeping," I explained. The platoon sergeant looked at the squad leader and both burst out laughing.

I was stunned. "Did I tell a joke?" I thought.

"He was just fucking with you, man. That's just the way he is," said the sergeant.

I was hoping that my complaint would go through the chain of command and that Private Williams would be placed on extra duty, but nothing happened to him. During the hike, Private Williams approached me.

"Hey, nigga, why the fuck did you tell Sarge, man? I was just fucking with you," he said. I was still upset. I ignored him. Private

Williams walked away and joined two other black soldiers, who were soon laughing and looking at me.

In the barracks, I was ostracized by the black troops and ignored by almost every white and Hispanic. Whenever the troops stayed in garrison, I was assigned latrine duties by the squad leader. One morning after chow, Lieutenant Walker from Battalion Headquarters came to the barracks. Someone called the troops to attention.

"I need a volunteer with a GT score of at least 110 to do clerical work at headquarters. Whoever is selected will be sent to clerical school for four weeks and be excused from all barracks duties. And will also be the colonel's driver," he said. About ten of us raised our hands. The lieutenant looked at each soldier from head to boots. Finally he returned to me.

"What's your GT score, soldier?" he asked.

"It's 122, sir," I snapped.

"Can anyone beat 122?" he asked. I looked left and right from the corner of my eyes. No one raised his hand.

"Follow me," said Lieutenant Walker. I followed him to the office. He pulled my file and saw the letter naming me best sentinel.

"Congratulations, I think I've made the right choice," he said.

After completing clerical training, I was assigned an office in Battalion Headquarters, working from nine to five. I was no longer ostracized and ignored by my peers.

"Don't fuck with him—he's the colonel's driver," the troops would say whenever I returned to the barracks from work. I enjoyed working with officers and thought about becoming an officer. I walked into Lieutenant Walker's office.

"Sir, what can I do to become an officer?" I asked.

"Why do you want to become an officer?" asked the lieutenant.

"Because officers are respected, they don't use bad language, and they don't use drugs. And I like being in the army," I said.

"You need a four-year degree, acceptance to officer candidate school, and you must be a United States citizen," said the lieutenant.

"Thank you, sir," I said, returning to my office, thinking that these qualifications were beyond my reach.

15 **Sunday morning** I put on my dress green uniform and went to a Catholic church on base. I observed several children receiving their First Communion during the mass. I began to think about going to catechism as a young boy. Florence's voice echoed in my head: "You think I'm gonna spend my money on a bedwetter like you so you can go to Communion?" I imagined shooting her with my M-16 and .45 caliber revolver again. Suddenly I began to sob. "Please God, forgive me for thinking about such a terrible thing," I whispered. At the conclusion of mass, I waited outside for the chaplain.

"Excuse me sir, Father. I would like to have a few words with you," I said. The chaplain smiled and shook my hand.

"What can I do for you?" he asked.

"I would like to have my First Communion. What should I do?" I asked shamefully.

"Oh, you want to become a Catholic?" asked the chaplain.

"No sir, Father, I am already a Catholic. I went to catechism as a young boy when I lived in Haiti. The day I was supposed to go to church to receive the sacrament, my mother told me that I could not go because she didn't have money to buy clothes," I explained, feeling uncomfortable. "Oh, I understand," said the chaplain.

"I know the catechism by heart. You can test me if you wish," I added. I followed the chaplain to his office. He gave me a few pamphlets to read and asked me for the name of my unit.

"If your unit will not be going out, come to see me Saturday at 1600 hours," said the chaplain. I shook his hand and felt as though a big load had been lifted from my shoulders.

When I returned the following Saturday, the chaplain baptized me. During the baptism, I recalled that I had already been baptized. It was a Friday morning because the cook had just returned from the market with fresh fish. I was about seven years old. That particular morning, Florence came home from church with a tall dark-skinned priest in a creamy white robe. The two sat on the front porch for a moment and then she invited him inside for coffee. He removed his robe, placed it on the back of a chair, and followed Florence into the bedroom. After a while he came out and put his robe back on. Florence was standing behind him. I was sitting on the front steps, killing ants with my fingers. On his way out, the priest smiled at me.

"Will you baptize him for me?" asked Florence.

"Certainly," answered the priest and went back inside. Florence waved me into the dining room.

The priest removed his black rosary from his pocket, placed it around his neck and asked Florence for a glass of water.

"What is your name?" asked the priest.

"Bobby," answered Florence before I could open my mouth.

"Bobby, I baptize you in the name of the Father, the Son, and the Holy Spirit," said the priest, dipping his finger into the glass and making a cross on my forehead.

After the sacrament, Florence looked at me and said, "I am your godmother, and the father is your godfather."

Before I walked out, the army chaplain gave me instructions for my First Communion.

"I'll see you tomorrow at 0900 hours," said the chaplain.

Sunday morning I wore my dress green uniform and shiny black boots. As I walked out of the barracks, Private Williams, who now called me "Frenchy," yelled out of the second-floor window.

"Hey, Frenchy, where the fuck you goin', man?" I looked up at him with a big grin and shouted back, "I am going to have my First Communion."

As I sat in church waiting for the sacrament, I visualized myself as the little excited boy restavec who once dreamed of wearing a white shirt, white pants, and a little red bow tie for his First Communion. But now the excitement that I had felt as a child after the final week of catechism did not return. Instead I felt empty, alone, and cold inside.

After Communion I went to the PX, bought a box of cookies, and returned to the barracks. I ate a few and distributed the rest among the troops without telling them what I was celebrating.

Because of the drugs, I stayed out of the barracks as much as possible, spending my free time in the gym or in a martial arts school conducted by a green beret sergeant.

One Friday afternoon, the troops had just received their pay. One of the sergeants came to the barracks, carrying a duffel bag under his arm. He unlocked the door to his room and walked in. Suddenly three soldiers left the bay and went to the sergeant's room. After a short while, one Pfc came out with a bulging pillowcase and went back to his bunk. Then he opened his locker and pulled out a box of Ziplock bags.

"Hey, Lockhart, go watch the door," he said to a buddy, as I watched him dump a big pile of dried green leaves on his bed. He rubbed the leaves in his hands and filled up all the plastic bags.

"Hey, Frenchy, you want a nickel bag?" he asked.

"No, thank you," I answered. The soldier arranged all the small bags in the pillowcase and left the barracks.

Monday morning at 0400 hours, the troops were awakened by the slamming together of two garbage can lids like cymbals by the sergeant.

"Wake up and get your nasty asses cleaned up," he shouted.

The soldiers were to take part in a week-long live-fire exercise off the base. It was cool and dark outside. Weapons, ammunition, and C rations were being distributed. The troops started packing. I folded my poncho while observing a shirtless Private Williams standing in front of his locker with his head and arms inside of it. After a short while, he slipped a small cigar box in his rucksack and sat in his bunk. His eyes were bloodshot. Small droplets of sweat were rolling down from his brow to his jaw like early morning dew on tall blades of grass. Everyone was combat-ready.

"Okay, we're moving out," yelled a sergeant. Private Williams put on his shirt and picked up his weapon. We were trucked to the airfield, where we put on our parachutes and waited to climb aboard a C-141 aircraft. Jeeps and tanks were being loaded in huge planes called C-5s. We finally boarded the plane. The jump went well. There were no casualties. The parachutes were left in the grassy field to be collected by riggers.

At the firing range, the order was given to load the weapons and to keep them on safety. I inserted a magazine into my M-16. Private Williams took his position and inserted a belt of ammunition in his M-60 machine gun.

"Commence firing," shouted the sergeant. We were moving and shooting. Private Williams stopped. His weapon had jammed. He turned his M-60 on its butt and kicked down the retracting handle while his head hung over the barrel. The weapon went off. Private Williams' head exploded as his body dropped lifelessly to the ground.

"Stop firing! Medic!" shouted the squad leader. Some soldiers vomited; others looked away. The medic rushed over with his backpack and covered the body with a poncho.

Later that day, a short mass was conducted by a chaplain. An M-16 rifle mounted with a bayonet was planted in the ground with a pair of shiny black boots to the side. A bugler played taps, and after the ceremony everyone was dismissed to his respective unit.

Returning to the barracks on Saturday night, we cleaned our weapons and turned them in. In the shower everyone had a bar of soap on a rope because no one wanted to bend down to pick up soap while naked.

"Hey, Frenchy, you wanna go to Fayetteville?" asked a soldier.

"Okay, I'll go with you," I answered. Once downtown, everyone went his separate way. I went to a Chinese restaurant for egg rolls and egg foo yong and then to a kung fu movie. By midnight I was back in my bunk. The barracks were empty.

Monday morning a number of troops went on sick call. It seemed that everyone had the same sickness: gonorrhea. I too asked permission to go to the clinic.

"What the hell's wrong with you, Frenchy?" asked the sergeant. "You never went on sick call."

"I am having problems with my stomach, Sarge," I said.

"You mean you've got the shits?" asked the sergeant.

"Yes, Sarge," I answered.

When I got to the clinic, it was packed with young soldiers waiting in a long line to be seen.

"If you're here for gonorrhea treatment, follow the yellow line," said a nurse. I misunderstood "gonorrhea" for "diarrhea" and followed the yellow line. When my number was finally called, I went into a small room where a nurse was waiting.

"When was your last sexual contact?" she asked.

"What?" I said, thinking that stomach problems shouldn't have anything to do with sex.

"When was the last time you had sexual intercourse?" she repeated. Since I was too embarrassed to say over a year ago, I answered, "Last week."

"Are you dripping?" she asked.

"Yes," I answered, thinking of my liquid bowel movements.

"Drop your pants," ordered the nurse, reaching for a cotton swab.

"I am not dripping now, there's nothing to see," I replied, wondering why she wanted a sample.

"When did you drip last?" asked the nurse.

"Last night and early this morning," I answered nervously.

At that point, the nurse was getting irritated and impatient. She snapped at me, "When are you going to be dripping again?" My stomach growled. "Soon," I answered, wondering why she was so upset.

"Go in the waiting room. When you think you're gonna be dripping again, come and let me know," said the nurse. I walked out and waited. After a few minutes I went back to summon the nurse, but she was seeing another soldier. I went to the bathroom and relieved myself. Instead of flushing the toilet, I dropped the lid and stood by the door. When her patient came out, I went back to see her.

"Nurse, I have just dripped," I said.

"Okay, now drop your pants and let me take a look," said the nurse.

"No, it is in the toilet," I said.

The nurse followed me to the bathroom.

"This I've got to see," she said.

"It is in there," I said, pointing to the toilet. She lifted the lid and dropped it.

"Shit, you don't have gonorrhea, you have the runs. Who let you in the army anyway?" snapped the nurse. I was directed to another section and given medication.

When I returned to work at headquarters, I found a handwritten letter on my desk to be typed. It read:

Dear Mr. and Mrs. Williams,
   It is with deep regret that I inform you of the accidental death of your beloved son Pvt. John D. Williams. . . .

Pvt. Williams was an outstanding soldier who served his country well. . . . The Army will miss him.

I typed the letter and placed it on Lieutenant Walker's desk for the colonel's signature, wondering how Private Williams had served his country well.

During formation that afternoon, the company commander pinned corporal stripes on my shirt collar.

"Congratulations, soldier, you've made corporal." I saluted and felt proud of myself. I thought about calling Florence and Denis in upstate New York to share my excitement with them. I went to the pay telephone, dialed the number, and hung up as someone said "Hello?" I walked into the sergeant's office and requested a five-day leave of absence.

"Where the hell're you going? I didn't think you had a home to go to," said the sergeant.

"I am going to visit my father in Haiti," I said, thinking that my accomplishments were good enough to earn me a place in my father's life. I wanted to establish a connection that would fill the void in my chest. I wanted Philippe to see me with the eyes of a father.

My leave was soon approved. I went to the bank, withdrew a thousand dollars from my savings, and went shopping at the PX. I bought a big suitcase and filled it with gifts of all sorts. I had the salesperson gift-wrap an electric shaver and two watches.

"What father would not be proud of a son who is a corporal and a paratrooper in the United States Army? When he sees me in uniform, he's going to welcome me with open arms and he's going to love my gifts," I said to myself.

My boots were glass-shined, my airborne wings sparkled like diamonds, and my suit was well pressed. I was ready for the inspection of my life.

During the flight to Haiti, I sat erect like a robot so as not to wrinkle my uniform. After landing, I went to the lavatory in the aircraft and double-checked myself in the mirror. At the airport in Port-au-Prince, it seemed like everyone was staring and pointing at me like I had just landed from another planet. I felt like a visitor without a country. I happened to be a soldier in the American army who knew only the Canadian national anthem but who had never lived in Canada. In my soul though, I was still Haitian. I commanded a taxi to 18 Rue Bernard and sat in the backseat like a VIP. When the driver stopped in front of the house, I removed my handkerchief and dusted off my boots. My heart was palpitating. The driver carried my suitcase all the way to the front door. I paid him ten times the fare. The driver shook with excitement and ran back to his car saying "Merci, bon Dieu, merci eternel."

I knocked. A maid opened the door and asked in Creole, "Who do you want?" with bright eyes.

"Monsieur Sébastien," I replied.

"Come in," she said, staring at me. I walked in and stood in the living room nervously with my suitcase beside me. After a short while, Philippe appeared.

"Oh, it's you. You're in the army?" asked Philippe.

"Yes, I am in the United States Army," I answered.

"How long are you here for?" asked Philippe. Without answering the question, I quickly opened my suitcase and pulled out the wrapped gifts and handed them to Philippe. Then I pulled out everything else and placed it all on the couch, trying to impress him.

"I am going out of town for a few days. You may stay," said Philippe.

"May I go with you?" I asked.

"Non," answered Philippe. I stayed for three days and felt more like a tolerated guest than a relative. Philippe's mother had died two years earlier. I never knew his father. I found myself alone most of the time. When Philippe returned, he drove me to the airport and this time he shook my hand and said good-bye.

I boarded the plane feeling disappointed. The void in my chest seemed to have gotten bigger, and my heart felt like a rock in the middle of a cold and empty cave. I felt like I had not passed inspection and had not accomplished my mission.

Returning to Fort Bragg, I bought a used car and took long drives on weekends to get away from the barracks.

Headquarters received news from the Pentagon that all combat units were to be placed on alert. The energy crisis of 1973 had begun, and we were facing the possibility of going to war in the

Middle East. I learned that the oil-rich nations of the Persian Gulf had boycotted the United States, causing a serious shortage of gasoline. I thought we would invade Kuwait and Saudi Arabia to solve the crisis. Two clerks from Division Headquarters came to the company to update personnel files. Every soldier was asked the same question: Who is your beneficiary in case you die in combat?

"I want the army to keep my insurance money if I don't make it back alive," I said.

"Seriously, you must give me the name of your beneficiary," said the clerk.

"I am serious. I don't have anybody and I want the army to use the money to buy more weapons," I explained, thinking that since the army was taking care of me, I had to take care of the army in return.

"Okay, I'll put the United States Army as your beneficiary," said the clerk.

During the afternoon formation, the company commander told the troops to stay combat-ready until further notice. Two soldiers from my platoon went AWOL. At 0500 hours, thousands of combat-ready troops were at the airfield with their parachutes, waiting for the word "Go" from the Pentagon. By 1500 hours that same day, the alert was called off and the troops were driven back to the barracks. I took my car for a drive. On a long deserted road on the base, I began to speed. Tears were flowing down my cheeks.

"What's wrong with me? Why is it that nobody wants me? What am I living for?" I shouted. I looked ahead at a huge tree on the side of the road and purposely crashed against it. I lost consciousness. The car was wrapped around the tree. I was awakened by a paramedic and driven to a military hospital. My X rays showed no broken bones.

"Were you trying to commit suicide?" asked an MP.

"No, I was not. I lost control of the car," I replied. After a short stay in the hospital, I was released and given a note suggesting bed rest for five days. In the barracks I was constantly breathing marijuana smoke. I ignored the doctor's recommendations and reported back to work. My mind was preoccupied with the drug problem. After work I visited the CID's office—the Criminal Investigation Division, the army's version of the FBI. I was greeted by a warrant officer.

"What can I do for you?" he asked.

"I want something done about a serious drug problem in the barracks," I said.

"Have you told this to your commanding officer?" asked the warrant officer.

"No, I don't want to go through the chain of command because the platoon sergeant is one of the distributors," I said.

"Give me his name and unit," said the warrant officer.

"Staff Sergeant Johnson, Company C, 1st Battalion, 325th Infantry," I said nervously.

"Where does he usually keep the drugs?" asked the warrant officer.

"Sometimes on paydays he distributes from his office. Other times from his house," I said.

"Have you ever been to his house?" he asked.

"Never, but most of the soldiers have," I answered.

"Can you get the guys to take you to his house?" he asked.

"That would be impossible. They don't trust me because I don't smoke," I replied.

"Smoke a joint with them to gain their trust or pretend that you smoke. We want him and his suppliers," said the warrant officer. I thought for a moment, biting my fingernails.

"It's against army regulations to use illegal drugs," I said.

"Sometimes you have to violate the law in order to enforce it. That's what undercover work is all about. To gain someone's trust you have to act like that person and do what he does," explained the warrant officer.

"I'll think about it," I said.

"Don't take too much time. We have to move fast on this. Here, take my card and give me a call tomorrow. There's someone I want you to meet," said the warrant officer.

"I'll call you tomorrow before noon," I said, leaving the CID's office. On my way to the barracks, I stopped at the PX and bought a six-pack of beer. As I walked into the bay, I opened a beer and pretended to be drunk.

"Hello, everybody! Anyone like to have a beer with me?" I asked.

"Yea, give me a fucking beer," said a white soldier.

"Hey, everybody, look at Frenchy. He's drinking beer. I thought he was a fucking saint, man," said another. The beer was quickly distributed. As the guys were drinking, I went to the bathroom and dumped my beer in the urinal. When I returned to the bay, someone handed me a joint.

"I am a drinker, not a smoker, and I am too drunk to smoke," I said as I threw myself on the bed.

"Frenchy's all right, man. I thought the nigga was a mother fuckin' saint," said a voice.

The next day, I called the warrant officer from headquarters. An appointment was set for 1900 hours. I met with the warrant officer and a civilian detective. I told them about the beer. "I think they are beginning to trust me now," I said.

"Payday is in two weeks. You have to get the guys to take you to Sergeant Johnson's house. Once you see drugs, give an excuse to leave the house. We'll be somewhere across the street, waiting for your signal," explained the detective, giving me his card.

"Okay, I'll take off my beret if I saw drugs," I said.

"If they agree to take you, before you leave the barracks give me a call," said the detective, shaking my hand. As I was about to walk out the door, the detective gave me money to buy more beer. I returned to the barracks with two six-packs. Once again I pretended to be drunk and distributed the beer.

Weekend before payday, I went to Fayetteville with the guys. In a bar I ordered beer and dumped it in the toilet.

On the evening of payday, the guys were getting dressed. "Where are you guys going?" I asked. They looked at each other.

"Frenchy's all right, man," said a black soldier.

"You wanna come with us?" asked the other.

"Yea," I answered.

"Get dressed, nigga. We ain't gonna wait," said the other black soldier.

"Okay, let me get my laundry," I said. I went to the telephone downstairs and called the detective. "It's all set!" I said and hung up. I picked up my clothes from the dryer and went back upstairs. I quickly got dressed and left with two black Pfcs and a white corporal. I found it odd that while the black Pfcs called each other "nigga," their white friend would not use the word, and when I tried to fit in by calling the white corporal "nigga," he didn't seem to like it.

We took a bus downtown and walked four blocks to a trailer park. The corporal knocked on a door and Sergeant Johnson opened up. He was sweating heavily and seemed surprised to see me. The trailer was lavishly decorated. The gold shag carpet felt like pillows under my feet. The air-conditioning was humming softly in the living room window. Four black girls, dressed like prostitutes, were sitting on the couch watching the *Lawrence Welk Show*. I was nervous. Sergeant Johnson brought two chairs from the kitchen to the living room. Everyone took a seat in front of the TV.

"Where's the bathroom, Sarge?" I asked nervously.

"Second door to your right," he said, pointing to the narrow corridor. Instead of going to the bathroom, I tried to open two other doors. They were locked from the inside. My heart was racing. I returned to the living room and sat next to a girl in a skintight leopard print skirt. Her long blond wig contrasted with her mahogany complexion. She smiled at me and slowly licked her upper lip. I returned the smile and directed my attention to the television. Suddenly Sergeant Johnson motioned with his head for me to follow him into the kitchen.

"She likes you, man—she wants you bad. Go to the bedroom in the back and I'll send her to you. Give her twenty-five dollars when you're done," he said.

"I have a girl, Sarge. I promised her that I wouldn't be with anybody else," I said. A tall black man came out of a room.

"Give me two nickels," he said. Sergeant Johnson went to a room, came back out with two small plastic bags of marijuana, and handed both to him on his way out. Suddenly a girl walked out of one of the back rooms and sat in the living room. The two Pfcs went in the back and were soon followed by two girls.

"I have to go now, Sarge. My girl is waiting for me," I said, removing my beret from my belt.

"I'll see you Monday morning," said Sergeant Johnson. I put on my beret at the door and stepped out. As I walked down the street, I noticed the detective sitting behind the wheel of a white Chevrolet. I removed the burgundy beret for a few seconds and put it back on my head.

Returning quickly to the garrison, I went to see a movie to distract my mind.

After the show, I returned to the barracks with anxiety, hoping the soldiers would not suspect me as the snitch. At 2100 hours, the lights went off. I could not sleep. I was afraid for my life. At 0500 hours, the troops were awakened by the sound of garbage can lids slamming together. I looked for the three soldiers. They were not in the bay. During formation, the squad leader reported four soldiers unaccounted for. After exercise, the troops went to chow. I reported to work at headquarters.

At 1700 hours, I returned to the barracks. The three soldiers were waiting for me.

"Motherfucker, you set us up, didn't you?" said the corporal, waving his hand at my face. I was surrounded. The three soldiers were closing in.

"Nigga, I thought you were a brotha," said a black Pfc.

"Are you a fucking CID man?" asked the other.

I was terrified. "If any of you touch me, I will tell the colonel and you will be court-martialed," I said.

"He's a fucking CID working undercover as the colonel's driver," said the corporal. Suddenly the squad leader walked in. I went to my locker and discovered the lock had been cut. My stereo and collection of the Beatles' records were missing. One Pfc pointed his index finger at me like a gun. I left the barracks and telephoned the detective.

"They know," I said.

"Get out of there and go to the CID's office," said the detective. I picked up my duffel bag and left the barracks. The warrant officer sent me to another unit on the other side of the base to spend the night. The next morning, my commanding officer sent for me at headquarters.

"What's going on?" he asked.

"Sir, I was trying to break up a drug ring in the barracks and now my life is in jeopardy," I answered.

"You have orders to leave immediately for Fort Lewis, Washington," said the C.O. After that meeting, I bought another car with my insurance money and drove to Tacoma, Washington.

16 **At Fort Lewis, Washington,** I reported to a non-airborne unit, or a "leg unit."

"I see that you've been to clerical school," said the first sergeant, looking at my personnel file.

"Yes, First Sergeant," I answered.

"Battalion Headquarters needs an S-2 clerk. Report to Lieutenant McKay," he said. I went to headquarters.

"Corporal Cadet reporting for duty, sir," I said, saluting the lieutenant. Lieutenant McKay returned the salute.

"You look sharp, Corporal," he said.

"Thank you, sir," I replied.

In the S-2 office were two desks and a big safe. The lieutenant assigned me the desk closer to the safe, opened it, and handed me a stack of documents stamped "Secret."

"I'll show you how to log and sort," said the lieutenant. After the first week, I learned the office's routine and was in charge whenever the lieutenant was absent.

One day after chow, a colonel walked in to inspect the office. I snapped to attention.

"At ease, Corporal. Show me your log," said the colonel.

"May I see your identification card, sir?" I asked.

"You're very sharp, Corporal," said the colonel, handing me his ID card.

"Thank you, sir," I answered, feeling proud.

"I detect an accent. Where are you from, Corporal?" asked the colonel.

"I am from Haiti, sir," I answered, feeling embarrassed.

"I assume you are a naturalized citizen," said the colonel.

"No, sir, I am not a citizen, but I intend to be," I answered.

"Are you telling me that you're not an American citizen and you're handling military secrets?" asked the colonel with a concerned look on his face.

"I did not know that I had to be an American citizen to work in S-2, sir," I replied.

"How long have you been handling military secrets, soldier?" asked the colonel.

"About two months, sir," I answered.

"I am afraid you can't work here any more," said the colonel, whose face was now turning red. He went to see the battalion commander and I returned to the barracks.

"Why didn't you tell me that you were not a U.S. citizen?" asked the first sergeant.

"I never thought about it," I answered.

"The colonel told the general, who called Immigration and a federal judge. I think you're about to become a U.S. citizen sooner than you think," said the first sergeant.

"I want to become a U.S. citizen, Sarge," I said.

"In the meantime, report to the platoon sergeant," said the first sergeant. Life in the barracks at Fort Lewis was no different from that of Fort Bragg. Every night after work and every weekend a few soldiers got together to smoke marijuana. I found myself saying constantly, "No, man, I don't smoke."

While at the PX one Friday afternoon, I noticed a sharply dressed white soldier with glass-shined boots. His black beret rested neatly on the right side of his crew cut. I approached him.

"Excuse me, are you stationed here?" I asked.

"Yea, I am with the 75th Rangers," answered the corporal.

"How can I join your unit?" I asked.

"Call the first sergeant and tell him that you want to be a Ranger. He might call you in for an interview. If he likes you, he'll tell the CO, and you'll get your orders to join," explained the Ranger. First thing Monday morning, I told my platoon sergeant.

"Sarge, I want to join the Rangers. I'd like permission to call their first sergeant," I said.

"You don't wanna join the Rangers. They spend more time in the woods than fuckin' snakes. Those guys are nuts, they train in the swamps," explained the platoon sergeant.

"I don't care; they look good," I said.

That morning I called the Ranger unit, and their first sergeant invited me in for an interview.

"Why do you want to be a Ranger?" asked the first sergeant.

"I am a paratrooper in a leg unit, and I miss jumping," I answered.

"What's your GT score?" he asked.

"It's 122," I answered. The first sergeant smiled.

"Do you smoke dope and use drugs?" he asked.

"Never," I answered.

"Congratulations, welcome to the 75th Rangers," he said, shaking my hand.

The Rangers were different from other units. They looked sharp, walked tall, and seemed proud of themselves. They treated each other with a kind of respect that seemed to solidify their esprit de corps, and their company commander always congratulated them for performance beyond the call of duty. The compound and the barracks reflected their attitudes about themselves. The walkways were lined with two columns of freshly painted white rocks. Not a single piece of debris could be found anywhere on the ground. The floor in the barracks was shined enough to shave on. A faint smell of wax was always noticeable in the air. In the mess hall, the cooks treated everyone like familiar paying customers.

Since I was the only black Ranger in the barracks, I never heard the word "nigga" again.

The following week, I was driven to a government building in Seattle, Washington, where a federal judge was waiting for me.

"Raise your right hand and repeat after me," said the judge. I complied with his request and repeated after him.

"Congratulations, you're now an American citizen," he said. I suddenly realized that I had inadvertently met half of the requirements to become an officer in the United States Army.

I went to the library for the first time, to inquire about colleges. I looked at the ranks of people in uniform and noticed that they were all officers. The librarian looked at me inquisitively.

"I would like to know what I need to do in order to get accepted to college," I said.

"Have you taken the SAT?" she asked.

"I am not familiar with it. What is it?" I asked.

"It's called the Scholastic Aptitude Test," she said slowly as if I were deaf and dumb.

"How can I study for it?" I asked. The librarian handed me a few booklets to read.

"These have sample questions and information about the SAT," she said. I began to visit the library regularly during my free time to prepare for the SAT. I was determined to become an army officer.

Around this time, my three years in the army were coming to an end. I was called into the first sergeant's office for a reenlistment talk.

"If you reenlist for four more years, Uncle Sam will give you a ten thousand dollar bonus and you'll make sergeant," said the first sergeant. I had no idea who Uncle Sam was and I didn't care to know.

"I want to go to college to become an officer," I said.

"Are you gonna try for ROTC?" asked the first sergeant.

"Yes," I answered, not knowing what ROTC stood for.

In the barracks I was sometimes teased because I had not taken any furlough, not even on holidays.

"Hey, Frenchy, you wanna go home with me for Thanksgiving? My mom's a great cook. You'll get a chance to meet my family," said Pfc Kelly, his voice full of pride. I accepted the invitation and we drove off to Oregon on a cool Wednesday afternoon. I wasn't worried about going to someone's house and staying overnight because I hadn't wet my bed in a very long time.

At the Kellys', I slept in a spare bunk in Pfc Kelly's room. His family was warm and friendly. Mrs. Kelly had been busy cooking and baking. The smell of pumpkin pie and cloves lingered in the house. The radio was playing country music. Every time Mrs. Kelly walked by her son, she made contact with him. A pat on the head, a shoulder rub, a friendly headlock, or a bright smile that seemed to say, "I love you. Welcome home, my son." Mr. Kelly, on the other hand, was busy showing his son the work he had done on the house and keeping him up to date on local events. Betty, Pfc Kelly's little sister, jumped on her brother's back for piggyback rides. The sight of all this affection made me feel uncomfortable, causing the void in my chest to feel even bigger. If there had been a gun available, I would have blown my head off while sitting in the family room. Whenever I found myself away from people, I would disappear deep into the backyard and sit on a tree stump behind the tool shed.

When dinner was about ready, the house was full of relatives. Pfc Kelly called me in to join his family and friends. At the dinner table, my hands began to shake. I kept my head down.

"Are you okay?" someone asked.

"I have a headache," I answered.

"Would you like to lie down?" asked Mrs. Kelly.

"Yes, please," I answered, excusing myself from the table. Everyone seemed concerned. I went into Pfc Kelly's room and then slipped through the back door. I went back behind the shed where I felt most comfortable.

I heard Pfc Kelly calling me. "Hey, Cadet, where are you?" I pretended not to hear him. He yelled again and louder.

"Over here," I finally answered.

"What's the matter with you? You're acting a little strange," he said.

"I'm okay now," I answered. Pfc Kelly seemed disappointed.

"My mom saved some dinner for you. Why don't you go eat?" he said. I went back in the dining room and ate alone as fast as I could. While the men watched football in the living room, the women were in the family room talking and preparing dessert. When I finished eating, I slipped back out again. Pfc Kelly called me back inside for the third time.

"Why can't you stay inside with us?" he asked.

"I don't know, I like to be outside," I answered.

"Come on, let's go inside. We're gonna have dessert now," he said. When I entered the family room, my presence seemed to transform the festivity into a wake. Mrs. Kelly tried to break the silence by passing around the family albums. I felt like I was sitting naked in front of all those people. I was trembling and sweat was running down my back. Someone passed an album to me and I kept it in my lap without opening it. I thought about Denis's and Florence's albums where I never saw a picture of myself. I thought about the mulatto taking pictures of Emilie with her dog. As Mr. Kelly took pictures of his son, daughter, and wife among the guests, I went to the bathroom so as not to have my picture taken.

Later, when Betty accidentally dropped a piece of pie on the floor, I sprang forward like a cat and picked it up. I then cleaned the spot on the carpet with a napkin. For a brief moment, I saw myself as the little restavec I once was, keeping the floor clean whenever there was a reception. Everyone seemed surprised.

"Thank you," said Betty. As I carried the dirty napkin out of the room, I let out a sigh of relief. I tried to remain in the kitchen as long as I could, but Mrs. Kelly coaxed me back into the family room.

"Well, Corporal, are you gonna make the army a career?" asked Mr. Kelly, trying to breath life back into the room.

"I want to become an officer," I answered glumly.

"That's a good move," replied Mr. Kelly. I nodded yes.

Mr. Kelly left the room and some people turned their attention to the small portable television set on the breakfast bar.

By late evening the guests were saying good-bye. Before bedtime, Pfc Kelly suggested leaving after breakfast in the morning.

Mr. and Mrs. Kelly came by the door of the bedroom and said goodnight. Everyone seemed awkward. Mrs. Kelly slowly closed the door. Pfc Kelly lay in bed facing the wall. I took a T-shirt from my bag and stuffed it in my underwear to absorb urine in case of an accident. I was awakened by the soaked T-shirt. The mattress was dry. I ate breakfast with the Kellys in silence and awkwardness.

During the drive back to Fort Lewis, Washington, the humming of the engine was the only sound in the car. The friendship between Pfc Kelly and me died a slow death.

17 **It was June of 1975.** My last two weeks in the army were emotionally tormenting. I worried about leaving the Rangers, the only safe home I had ever had. I went back to wetting my bunk. My desire to earn a four-year degree was stronger than my willingness to remain in the army as an enlisted man. I said good-bye to the troops and boarded a bus to the airport with my duffel bag across my shoulder.

I approached a ticket agent and told her that I wanted to go to a warm city with a college. The clerk seemed puzzled.

"Where exactly do you want to go?" she asked.

"I would like to go to a place where it does not snow and where there is a college. You see, I want to use my GI Bill to get a four-year degree," I said. The clerk's eyes got bigger as she listened to me.

"Do you have any idea what state or city you want to go to?" asked the clerk.

I thought for a moment. "I know that I do not want to go to New York. It is too cold there. But if you have a flight going to a warm place that has a college, you can put me on it," I said. The clerk checked the monitor in front of her.

"I have a flight leaving for Tampa, Florida. It's warm there. Do you want it?" she asked.

"Do they have a college in Tampa?" I asked.

"Yes, the University of South Florida is there, as well as several other community colleges," she explained.

"I will take it," I said.

After I paid for the ticket, two security officers approached me.

"Excuse me, young man, may I see your ID card?" said an officer.

"Yes sir," I answered, reaching for my wallet. I handed my ID to the officer.

"You just got out of the army?" he asked.

"Yes sir, and I am on my way to college," I said with a smile.

"Good luck, son," said the officer as he handed me back my ID card.

The plane landed late at Tampa International Airport. I rented a hotel room at the airport and stayed the night. Early in the morning, I looked through the telephone book for colleges and wrote down some addresses. I took a taxi and told the driver to take me to a cheap motel near Hillsborough Community College. I rented a room for two days and left my duffel bag. I then walked to the college and completed an application, leaving the address blank.

"You need an address," said the clerk.

"I am staying in a motel. I do not have an address yet," I said.

"You will not be considered for admission without an address," she explained.

"Where can I rent an apartment?" I asked. The clerk sent me to a bulletin board, where I found several roommate-wanted ads. I removed several ads and left the campus. On my way back to the motel, I stopped at a car dealer and bought an old 1963 Dodge Dart for $250. I needed an address fast because registration began in a few days. Going to breakfast at McDonald's early Sunday morning, I noticed a black woman with gray hair standing on the roadside next to her car. I pulled in behind her.

"Do you have car trouble, ma'am?" I asked.

"Yes, young man, I have a flat tire. I knew Jesus was gonna send somebody to help me," she said.

"Do you live far from here?" I asked, jacking up the car.

"No, I live near the college. Where do you live?" she asked.

"I am staying in a motel until I find a place. I am trying to get into college, but they will not accept my application without an address," I explained.

"How much are they charging you at the motel?" she asked.

"Twenty dollars a day," I answered.

"You can stay with me for forty dollars a week until you find a place, and I'll give you supper," she offered.

"I'll take it," I said. After I changed the tire, she followed me to the motel to get my duffel bag, and I followed her to her house.

Monday morning I returned to the college and registered for classes, using the woman's address on my application.

After living in her house for one full week, I began to look for apartments. I dialed a number. A young man answered.

"I found your ad on campus. Are you still looking for a roommate?" I asked.

"Yes, I am. The rent is two hundred a month, including utilities," answered the voice. He gave me directions to his apartment. I rang the doorbell. A young white man opened the door.

"I am here to see the room," I said.

"You didn't tell me you were black," said the young man.

"You did not ask," I replied, feeling confused.

"Don't get me wrong—it's not my fault. You should have told me in advance that you were black. I didn't ask because you don't even sound black. Don't think that I'm prejudiced—I'm not. But my parents are paying for the apartment, and they come to visit at least once a week. I don't think they will be comfortable with you as my roommate," he explained.

"I understand," I said, walking away.

I called several other roommate-wanted ads and each time I added, "I happen to be black. Will that be a problem?" They always replied, "Yes, it will." I couldn't understand why in civilian life no white person wanted to have a black roommate, whereas in the army the thirty white Rangers with whom I shared the bay had no objections—in fact, they all treated me like a brother. As a young black man, I found civilian life in the South very harsh. My blackness was an obstacle to obtaining the most basic necessities of life. A part-time job was harder to obtain than decent housing. While I felt like a soldier who was not properly trained to survive in enemy territory, most white people, it seemed, had been trained all their lives to see me as dumb, dirty, dishonest, devilish, and a threat to their security. I couldn't despise them, because in my black native land and environment I was conditioned to think of whites as intelligent, honest, caring, and godlike. Nonetheless, I avoided their bigotry and concentrated on reaching my goal.

One day I walked into a barbershop and sat down in a chair next to an elderly man to await my turn. I took a magazine from a small table and began to thumb through it. It didn't occur to me that I was the only nonwhite person in the room. Suddenly the sounds of scissors and electric clippers went dead, bringing a chilling silence to the shop. I felt a presence in front of me. I lowered the magazine and lifted my head. One of the barbers towered over me.

"May I help you?" he asked, straight-faced.

"I am here to get a haircut," I answered, thinking, Why else would I be in here?

"We don't cut you people's hair. You better get out of here right now," he said in a bellicose tone with the scissors firmly in his grip. Every pair of Caucasian eyes in the room was piercing me. Awkwardly I stood up. As I started to walk, my legs felt heavy and my shoulders burdened, and the front door seemed a mile away.

I rented a one-bedroom apartment for $350 per month and felt overcharged because of my race. I worked as a dishwasher during the late afternoon to supplement my GI Bill and spent many hours studying with the help of a French-English dictionary. I made C's and occasionally B's. Most of the professors had low expectations of me because of my race, whereas my professor at Ecole Jean-Charles in Haiti had high expectations of me because of my light skin.

One day, while I was having lunch in the school cafeteria, one of my professors came and sat next to me.

"Where are you from? I like your accent," he said.

"I am from Haiti," I replied.

"Are you going home for Christmas?" he asked.

"No, I'll be here," I answered, feeling ashamed that I had no home in my native land.

"I am having a Christmas party at my house. Will you be able to make it?" asked the professor.

"Thank you, I'll be there," I answered.

The professor gave me directions and I wrote them in my notebook.

At the professor's house, he answered the door and put his arm around my shoulder.

"Come on in, Jean. You made it," he said. As he introduced me to the guests and his family, he handed me a glass of eggnog.

"Sit down, make yourself at home," he said. I sat nervously on the couch next to a white lady. My knees were close together, my elbows in my lap, my back hunched, and my head down. I was trembling with glass in hand. Suddenly everyone stopped talking and directed their attention toward me.

"What's the matter, Jean? Are you all right?" asked the professor.

I stood up, placed my drink on the table, and walked toward the door.

"I have to go now," I stuttered as I ran out. Everyone was speechless. I went to my apartment and spent the holidays alone. When I returned to class, I avoided eye contact with the professor as much as possible. At the end of the class, as I was on my way out the door, he stopped me.

"I want to see you in my office right now," he said sharply. I followed him nervously to his office and he closed the door.

"What the hell was wrong with you at my house? You've embarrassed me and my family in front of all my friends," he said angrily.

"I am sorry, sir," I said.

"Sorry—you're sorry. Is that all you have to say? You try so hard in class. I was impressed by you. I invited you to my house. You humiliated me and my family, and now you're sorry?" said the professor, throwing his arms in the air.

"I don't know what to do or how to act when I am in a living room with people, because the people who raised me never allowed me to be in the living room unless I had to dust the furniture or clean the floor. I feel very uncomfortable sitting in living rooms with people," I explained.

"What kind of people were they? Are you kidding?" he asked.

"No sir, that's the truth," I said.

"Where are your parents?" asked the professor.

"My father, who is white, gave me to a woman because I was born black," I said.

"Where's your mother?" he asked.

"My mother died when I was about a year old. She was my father's cook," I said.

"The woman who raised you, was she black?" asked the professor.

"Yes, she is," I answered.

"How did you get to the United States?" he asked.

"When the woman who raised me came to this country, she abandoned me in Haiti. And my father, who didn't know what to do with me, sent me to live with her in New York," I answered.

"You need help and a lot of it. Have you ever seen a psychiatrist?" he asked.

"No sir," I replied, not knowing what a psychiatrist was.

"You should transfer to the University of South Florida. They have people who can help you," he suggested.

At the end of the term, I transferred to the University of South Florida and majored in international relations and French.

In my first international studies class, a tall, white-haired, distinguished-looking male professor dressed in a light-gray suit walked in. His red bow tie brought back painful memories of the day I was supposed to have my First Communion. The angry face of Florence flashed momentarily across my mind. I soon found solace in the professor's quick smile and receptive spirit. He introduced himself to the class as Dr. Mark T. Orr, chairman of the history department. I thought that a chairman must work with chairs, since a mailman delivers letters, a fireman puts out fires, a fisherman catches seafood, etc. etc. I became curious because he didn't strike me at all as a chairman. I raised my hand and asked, "Please tell me what do you do as a chairman."

"I have a department meeting after this class. Why don't you follow me and see for yourself?" he replied with that quick smile of his. After class, as I followed Dr. Orr through the long corridors, I visualized a woodshop where chairs were being made. To my surprise, he entered a room where several professors were waiting at a long oval-shaped table. Dr. Orr introduced me to the professors as if I were an honored guest and signaled me to sit next to him. I felt important yet awkward. After the meeting, he escorted me out and said, "That's what I do as chairman." His attitude fanned the spark of learning within me more than ever.

I visited the student health center and made an appointment to see a psychiatrist. When I returned to the health center, I sat nervously in the lobby waiting to be called. Finally a beautiful Hispanic woman appeared.

"Jean Cadet?" she said.

"Yes," I answered and followed her into her office.

"How can I help you?" she asked.

"My professor at the community college said I need help because I don't know how to conduct myself in living room situations," I replied.

"Why did he say you need help?" she asked.

I explained the incident at the Christmas party as well as the one in Pfc Kelly's house as the psychiatrist listened attentively.

"Tell me something about your childhood," she asked.

"When I was a restavec in Haiti, I was never allowed in the living room unless I had to dust the furniture or clean the floor," I began. Since she didn't know the meaning of the word *restavec*, I explained how the system worked. As the session went on, the psychiatrist began to ask more questions.

"What else did she make you do?" she asked.

"Once a month, she locked me in the bathroom and made me hand-wash the rags she used for her period," I continued. At that point, her mouth dropped open.

"What else?" she asked.

"I didn't know where the blood came from—I thought she was going to die," I said as tears began to blur my vision. The psychiatrist pulled out a tissue, wiped her own eyes, and handed the box to me.

"I want you to return in three days," she said, and made an appointment for me.

I had moved into a townhouse closer to USF. When I entered the front door, my roommate, Aaron, a foreign student, was on the telephone. I heard him say, "I love you too, Mom." Suddenly something snapped inside of me. I removed my book bag from my shoulder and threw it with rage against the wall, causing a portrait to fall down.

"What the hell's wrong with you, man?" yelled Aaron. I went into the kitchen screaming. I threw pots and pans out into the backyard and kicked the chairs.

Aaron called Emergency.

"My roommate is going nuts in the apartment. I don't know what's wrong with him," he said. I walked out and went on a long walk before Emergency arrived. When I returned to the apartment, I apologized to Aaron, who remained suspicious of me.

"The police were here. You scared me, man. What was wrong with you?" asked Aaron.

"I was mad at my mother," I replied, thinking of Florence.

That same night I began to have nightmares in slow motion, re-experiencing the horrific parts of the childhood I had described to the psychiatrist and wetting my bed. I thrashed and trembled in my sleep and dreamed that I was a little boy restavec being chased by a giant Florence, who was naked with a penis and carrying a broomstick. She caught me. As she was about to place a foot on my neck, my scream awakened me. My heart raced as I panted. That morning, on my way to class, I stopped at the ROTC office.

"I'd like to sign up for officer training," I said. I was given an application and told to return at the same time and date that I had an appointment with the psychiatrist. I could not decide at that moment whether to suspend the treatments or join the ROTC. I waited till the last moment and ripped up the application while waiting in the psychiatrist's office. The sessions drained me emotionally—I was sobbing during each one. The nightmares became routine.

Around this time, my landlord rented the third bedroom of the apartment I shared with Aaron. Our new roommate was a bearded, average-height white man named Ross, who must have been in his early to mid fifties. Late one evening, I noticed Ross reading a magazine named *Soviet Life* at the kitchen table. Suddenly I remembered that the U.S. Army had trained me to regard all communist nations as enemy countries. Then I recalled my conversation with Florence's cook in Haiti about the dead Kamokins who were dumped near the airport as a warning to anyone who might be a communist sympathizer. At that moment, I assumed that Ross was a domestic enemy of the United States, the country I loved. I thought about the oath I had taken the day I was shipped to Fort Dix for basic training. "I will support and defend the Constitution of the United States against all enemies, foreign and domestic" echoed in my mind.

In the morning, as soon as Ross left for work, I searched his room and discovered a big stock of *Soviet Life* magazines on his nightstand. I was convinced that he was indeed a domestic enemy. I picked up the telephone, dialed zero, and asked the operator for the local FBI office.

"This is the FBI, Agent McCain speaking," said a voice.

"My name is Jean-Robert Cadet. I am an army veteran and a student at the University of South Florida. My roommate is a communist," I said.

"How do you know he's a communist?" asked the agent.

"He has a big stack of *Soviet Life* in his room," I replied.

"What kind of work does he do?" asked the agent.

"He told me that he's a teacher," I replied.

"Does he do research at the university?" asked the agent.

"No, he teaches at a high school," I replied.

"Give me his full name and I'll check it out," said the agent.

I told the FBI agent everything I knew about Ross. From that day on, I listened to Ross's phone conversations and checked his mail for foreign stamps. I was sure that, because of my army training, I would be given the order to eliminate Ross. I waited expectantly, but the order never came. Eventually Ross moved out. I could not understand why this enemy had been allowed to get away until I was a senior, when I took a course on United States government and learned that the Constitution protects everyone's political preferences.

Making friends with young black American men my age was a challenging task. I tried to join the black fraternity, but they rejected me after the initial interview because, as they put it, "You don't talk like a brotha; you don't walk like a brotha; you ain't no brotha." When I tried the white fraternity, they looked at me as if I had lost my mind. However, the white female students were more receptive toward me. I would have joined their sorority had they accepted men. The three I had become friends with told me that I was different from American blacks. I assumed that it was because of my Caribbean accent.

I invited the dark-haired one who was in my international studies class to my apartment to discuss United Nations Resolution 242. She arrived on her bike with her books and notes at about eight-thirty in the evening. I had made chicken with rice for dinner. By eleven o'clock, there was a severe thunderstorm and I invited her to spend the night. She looked outside and reluctantly accepted my offer.

When it was time for bed, I gave her a new toothbrush and my only pajamas to wear. I showed her to my bedroom and apologized for not having a bed. Then I put fresh linens on the mattress and changed the pillowcase while she changed in the bathroom. I put on a pair of shorts and a T-shirt. She returned to the room, and I went to the bathroom to brush my teeth. Returning to the bedroom, I folded my old army jacket and used it as a pillow. I lay down, turned my back toward her, and switched off the lamp.

"Good night," I said.

"Good night," she replied. There was silence which was occasionally interrupted by thunder and lightning. Then I heard her let out a long sigh of relief.

In the morning, I made her breakfast and fresh orange juice. As we ate, she looked at me smilingly.

"You're not really a black guy," she said.

"What do you mean by that?" I asked.

"Well, you didn't try anything and you were so nice to me. Do you think I am pretty? Be honest!"

"You are very beautiful. You are my friend and I respect you," I said.

"Like I said, you're not a black guy, because I've never met a black guy who didn't try to force himself on me."

At the restaurant where I worked, I was finally promoted to waiter. One day a customer tipped me a ten-dollar bill. He was a tall black man about six feet, well groomed, and in his fifties. His businesslike appearance and his salt and pepper hair made him look distinguished.

"The service was superb," he told me.

"Thank you, sir. I hope you visit us again and soon," I replied.

It was almost midnight and the restaurant was about to be closed.

"Are you a student at the university?" he asked.

"Yes sir, I'm a senior," I answered proudly.

"I am retired. My name is Jeff Bronston. What is your name, young man?" he asked.

"I am Jean Cadet," I answered.

"Do you work every night?" he asked.

"No sir. Mondays and Tuesdays are my days off," I replied.

Wednesday night Mr. Bronston came to the restaurant again and asked to be seated in my section. Before he left, he gave me another ten-dollar bill and his business card.

"I like to help young ambitious people whenever I can," he said.

"Thank you, sir," I said. After a few weeks, I began to confide in Jeff, calling him at home at least once a week. Jeff promised to help me find a good job after graduation through his professional contacts.

I was happy to have found a father figure who seemed to care about me.

"If you ever need help with tuition, all you have to do is ask," offered Jeff. I was elated but never could find the courage to ask Jeff for money, although I was in need of tires and a battery for my sixteen-year-old Dodge Dart. Most of the time I relied on public transportation to get to work.

One Friday night Jeff came to dine. As usual he asked to be seated in my section.

"Can you give me a ride home after work?" I asked.

"Certainly. What happened to your car?" he asked.

"It wouldn't start," I replied. After work Jeff drove me home.

"I'll help you with the car in the morning. I'll see you around ten," said Jeff and drove off.

The next morning, Jeff showed up.

"Are you ready? Let's go—I have something to show you," he said. I got in his car, a black Lincoln Continental. He stopped at a BMW dealer and asked to test-drive their smallest model.

"Why don't you drive?" he said to me.

"Are you getting another car?" I asked.

"Yes, I need a second car—something smaller to drive around town," he said. On the way back to the dealer, Jeff asked to drive and told the salesman that he would return later.

"There's something else I want to show you," he said to me. He drove to a beautiful gated condominium complex. "This is where I live," Jeff said as he parked the car. I followed him inside and he showed me every room.

"How would you like to live here with me?" asked Jeff.

"Yes, I would. This is the most beautiful place I have ever seen," I said. Jeff sat on the couch and signaled me to sit next to him.

"You can move in today and I'll let you drive the BMW to school," he said. I was speechless and I felt uncomfortable.

"It's okay. You have nothing to worry about. I'll take care of you—all you have to do is be my friend."

As he said this, Jeff placed his hand on my thigh, stroking the skin beneath my shorts. I stood up.

"I want to go back home. I need to study for an exam," I said. Jeff, who sensed that I was uncomfortable, drove me back to my apartment. No one said a word in the car.

"If you change your mind, give me a call," said Jeff as I was getting out of the car.

I quit my job as a waiter to spend more time studying for my final exams.

18 **In my last session** with the psychiatrist, I expressed my fear of leaving the security of a college campus to face the job market.

"I have confidence in you. You'll do very well. But I think you should go to New York and confront Florence. Let her know how much she had hurt you," she said.

"During my three years in the army, every time I held a gun I saw Florence at the end of it. Every time I touched a bayonet, I saw myself stabbing her. And every time I drove a tank over a tree, I saw her lying on the ground. Yet every year after I joined the army, I bought her Christmas and Mother's Day cards. I chose the ones with the sweetest sentiments, I signed them and put stamps on them, but I could never find the courage to drop them in a mailbox," I said.

"Why did you buy them?" asked the psychiatrist.

"Because that is what a son is supposed to do for his mother," I answered.

"I don't think you're capable of killing anyone," she said.

"I don't know," I said, shrugging.

In June 1979, I received my last GI Bill check. My rent was overdue and I had been served with an eviction notice.

During graduation, I sat somberly in the auditorium thinking about where I was going to live. I looked around and saw smiling parents with pride in their eyes.

"Jean-Robert Cadet," called the dean of my college. I walked onstage, shook the dean's hand, received my diploma, and walked out.

I drove to my apartment and loaded my belongings in the trunk of my car. I showed up at the apartment of a friend, a young black woman who was working for the telephone company.

"Can I sleep on your couch until I get on my feet?" I asked.

"You don't have a job and you want to sleep on my couch and eat my food? No, I don't allow that, I'm sorry," she said.

For the next two weeks, I slept in my car and ate at fast-food restaurants until I found another job, as a room service waiter in a hotel. Through an acquaintance, I found an elderly woman named Alvina Jefferson who took me in as a boarder for sixty dollars a month. I immediately felt comfortable with her because she reminded me so much of Grannie Alcée, Florence's mother.

It was hot in Tampa one particular August day of 1979. By ten o'clock that morning, the temperature in the small wood-frame house was in the nineties. I sat on the front porch beside Mrs. Jefferson, who was fanning, rocking, and complaining about the heat. The fan she held in her aged hand bore the picture of Martin Luther King Jr. The shade of a big tree in the front yard provided some relief.

I didn't want to leave the house that morning because I had sent out nearly two dozen résumés and I didn't want to miss an invitation to a job interview. It took the eighty-two-year-old Mrs. Jefferson a long while to get off her chair to answer the telephone. Usually by the time she reached the front door, the caller had hung up. Around eleven o'clock, the telephone rang. I ran inside and answered it.

"May I speak to Jean Cadet?" asked the voice of a woman.

"This is he," I answered anxiously.

"This is Joyce Hughes from Citrus International. Mr. White would like to know if you could come in tomorrow at ten o'clock for an interview," she said. After I accepted the invitation, I brushed my only blue suit and took my shoes outside to shine them.

"You look so happy, did you get the job?" asked Mrs. Jefferson.

"No ma'am, not yet. They just want to interview me. I will get the job," I said with confidence.

"Do they know you're a colored man?" she asked.

"No ma'am," I said with diminished enthusiasm.

"Don't get your hopes too high. Crackers don't like to hire Negroes. They're N-A-S-T-Y," she said. Her face seemed like it had witnessed the days of slavery.

"There are some good white people, Mrs. Jefferson—I've met a few," I assured her, thinking of Mr. Rabinowitz, my history teacher at Spring Valley High School.

"If you find one, he will never pay you what you worth, boy," she said.

"I just want a foot in the door," I replied.

"When I did laundry for this Jewish family, I would fold them towels and they would count them in front of my face. They made me feel like a thief," she said angrily, spitting tobacco juice in a large tin can beside her chair. Then she chuckled.

"What's so funny?" I asked.

"I had been working all day cleaning house and washing clothes for this Jewish woman. I was dead tired, I tell you. I took the bus home and this little white girl got in and kept staring at me. Oh, she could've been thirteen or fourteen. We got off the bus together. She was still staring at me. I turned around and asked her why she was staring at me like that. She said, 'My mother got a dress just like yours, and when I get home I am gonna tell her and she's gonna burn it.' I was so damn mad, I told her to tell her mama that I got a p——y just like hers and she can burn that too. I tell you, that little white girl ran all the way home," said Mrs. Jefferson, laughing till there were tears in her eyes. Unlike Florence, who thought that white people could do no wrong, Mrs. Jefferson's attitude toward whites was so bitter I couldn't have invited a white friend into her house. She was especially bitter toward the police, and every time she saw a squad car drive by her house she said, "Look at them crackers. They're restless. They must be looking for some niggers to beat."

The following day I drove to Citrus International carrying a notepad and a pen. I walked into the lobby of the two-story building and introduced myself to the white receptionist. She dialed a number and announced my arrival. Soon a blond secretary walked down the steps and escorted me to Mr. White's office. He introduced himself as the general manager and immediately inquired about my knowledge of the French language. "I am from Haiti," I said, feeling ashamed that I was born in a country that is synonymous with extreme poverty and political instability—a country whose government allows the continuation of child slavery under the label of restavec.

Throughout the interview, my heart was pounding. I couldn't believe that I, a former restavec, was in a corporate office being interviewed for the position of assistant vice president of export. Mr. White offered me ten thousand dollars a year to work as an export assistant and assistant to the honorary French consul. I was so impressed with job titles, I agreed to his offer. I shook hands with Mr. White, but I walked out of his office feeling discouraged. I realized I had accepted the position with the mentality of a slave.

"I should have negotiated with him," I said aloud in the car driving home. I was making more money working as a waiter six hours a day.

Arriving at Mrs. Jefferson's house, I parked the car under the tree. She was fanning, rocking, and chewing tobacco. She spat in the tin can.

"Did you get the job?" she asked.

"Yes ma'am," I answered glumly.

"You don't look like you got the job," she added.

"Oh, it's the heat, Mrs. Jefferson, it's the heat," I replied, thinking about her remarks that the white man will never pay a Negro what he's worth. I didn't want to fuel her anger at the white man by telling her the reason for my long face, for she would have started by attacking every institution in Tampa again. I knew that first she would tell me about the judge who had given her friend five years in prison for a robbery he didn't commit or the hospital that denied treatment to its own black cleaning crew. Then she would talk about the cracker police beating Negroes.

When I reported to work the next morning, I was introduced to an elderly gentleman named José Fernández, a Cuban immigrant who had been with the company for a few years. José told me with great pride that he used to be a officer in the Cuban navy under Batista. I was not impressed because he was not telling me about a branch of the U.S. military. "Big deal. I used to be a Ranger in the U.S. Army," I said to myself.

"This is a good company. I started as an export assistant just like you," said José. I wanted to ask him what his starting salary was, but it was against company policy for employees to discuss their salaries. I learned the export business along with its unethical practices so well that I could have started my own trading company. I worked an average of fifty hours a week and my biweekly pay was less than four hundred dollars.

José always smiled at his paycheck before he put it in his blazer that he hung on the hat rack in a corner of the office. As soon as he went to the men's room, I searched his pocket to verify his salary. It was four times my amount. I was so perplexed, I lost my concentration and was unable to send a telex to a customer in Paris.

Later that day, I confronted the company's accountant with my paycheck and told him that I had worked fifty hours a week and deserved overtime pay.

"You're a salaried employee. You'd get the same amount no matter how many hours you worked," he said.

"I would like to get paid by the hour," I replied.

"I will have to get Mr. White's authorization before I can do that," he said.

When I returned to work the next day, the accountant handed me a notepad. "Mr. White wants you to keep track of your overtime hours. At the end of each week, get José to sign the sheet before you turn it into payroll," he said.

It was a company of good ol' boys. The only black employee besides me was the janitor. When work was slow, the good ol' boys would get together to tell each other "nigger jokes." The latest jokes were sometimes told to the general manager first. He would walk around with a big grin on his face, savoring the aftertaste.

On my way to the men's room, I overheard a salesman telling a joke about a traffic accident. "This good ol' boy rear-ended a car at a red light. When an officer arrived at the scene, he talked to the good ol' boy first. He said, 'How fast was that nigger backing up when he ran into you?'" They all burst out laughing until tears formed in their eyes. I shared in their laughter, because at that time I didn't have the soul of an American black man to feel the impact of the word *nigger* when uttered by whites.

Little by little, my black Haitian soul was being Americanized. It happened gradually, through experiences that I never sought and through the process of adaptation—the way animals changed their appearances to adapt and survive in hostile environments.

It all began to happen at nine o'clock one hot and muggy night on Hillsborough Avenue. I had just moved out of Mrs. Jefferson's house and into a two-bedroom apartment that I was sharing with a young white man who answered my advertisement. I was trying to beat a traffic light in a black section of town while driving home. A police cruiser was a good distance behind me. I panicked and made a sharp left turn into a dark parking lot, trying to hide from the police. I turned off the headlights and waited in the car. The cruiser pulled in behind me with flashing lights. I was shaking with fear. The voice of Mrs. Jefferson echoed in my head: "They must be looking for some niggers to beat up."

Two white officers—a tall man and a woman—approached my car. The woman shined a flashlight in my face from the passenger side. The male officer stood by my door searching the backseat.

"Hey, boy, do you make it a habit a going through red lights?" he asked, emphasizing "boy." As I tried to move my head to make eye contact with him, he poked the side of my face with a hard object.

"Don't you move, boy. You haven't answered my question yet."

"I thought the light was yellow when I went through it," I replied, frightened like a cornered cat.

"You don't know your colors, do you B-O-Y?" he asked.

"Yes sir, I do sir," I replied.

"License and registration," he snapped.

I gave him the documents and the two of them returned to their car. After a long moment, they returned to my car and the beam of a flashlight reoccupied my face. I signed for the citation and turned on my ignition. As I was backing up, the policeman suddenly walked behind my car as if he were daring me to hit him. I quickly stepped on the break pedal, avoiding him by inches.

"What's the hurry, nigger?" he shouted, offering me one last opportunity to fulfill his wish, but I was determined not to get beat up. That was the first time a white man called me "nigger," and the word had the same effect on me that "restavec" did when I was a boy. It felt like a hard punch in the gut that knocked the wind out of my lungs.

At Citrus International, I waited for the busiest time to ask for a raise.

"My responsibilities have increased, and I need new clothes," I said to my boss. Mr. White looked at me for a minute or two and took a deep breath.

"Let me tell you something, young man. This company is eighty years old and we never had a black in your position before. Don't rock the boat," he said. I walked out of his office feeling numb. I returned to my office and waited for a Mrs. Roy, who had an appointment to see the French consul. Andrea, the department secretary, came in and announced the arrival of Mrs. Roy.

"Please show her in," I said. Mrs. Roy walked in and I stood up to greet her.

"I am here to see the French consul," she said.

"I am the assistant to the French consul. What can I do for you?" I asked.

"You can't help me because my document is in French. Only the French consul can help. You're colored—you don't know any French," she snapped.

"Ma'am, the French consul doesn't speak French. I am his assistant. I handle all of his affairs," I said.

"I am not that desperate. I can get somebody else," she replied, walking out. I took a deep breath and maintained my composure.

Mr. Smith, the French consul, was a good ol' boy. Since he was about to retire, I was hoping he would recommend me to the general consul in New Orleans to succeed him. I thought that title would definitely impress my father, thus assuring me a place in his heart. But when the time came, Mr. Smith selected a good ol' boy to replace him and retained me as the new appointee's assistant.

On the eve of Thanksgiving, Harry, my roommate, approached me with a request.

"Hey, Jean, do you have any plans for Turkey Day?" he asked.

"No, I have nothing planned," I answered, thinking that he was about to invite me to his parents' house for dinner.

"Could you do me a favor?" asked Harry.

"What's the favor?" I asked.

"My parents are coming here for Thanksgiving and they're bringing the food. They don't know that you're black and my dad will not break bread with blacks. Will you disappear for a few hours? I'll tie a string on the doorknob to let you know if they're still here," said Harry.

"What time would you want me out?" I asked, feeling like a little restavec again.

"They're coming at twelve. You can leave about eleven," said Harry. At about eleven o'clock, Harry went out to buy ice. I was about to go to Morrison's Cafeteria, where I ate Thanksgiving dinner every year, when the doorbell rang. I opened the door. Six people were standing outside. Before I could say anything, an elderly man said, "Sorry, we have the wrong door," as he tried the next apartment. I closed the door and went back inside. A short while later the doorbell rang again. I opened it.

"The woman next door told us that our Harry lives in this apartment. Who are you?" asked Harry's father.

"My name is Jean. I live here and Harry is my roommate," I said.

"Where is he?" he asked.

"He went to the store. He should be back any moment," I said. Everyone walked in with baskets and bags of food. Harry's mother rearranged the furniture and set the table. I was about to walk out, but the smell of the food convinced me to stay. Harry walked in. He stared at me with surprise.

"They came as I was leaving," I whispered, raising my shoulders. I went to my room and sat on the bed. I purposely left the door open to hear the conversation in the living room.

"You never told me you had a colored for a roommate," said the father.

"Sorry, Dad. But we don't socialize. He works days and I work nights," explained Harry.

"Okay, everyone, the table is ready," said the mother. Everyone was quiet except for the sound of utensils against the plates. My stomach growled.

"Maybe they think I left the apartment," I said to myself. I coughed three to four times and waited for an invitation. Finally I walked out of my room, past the dining room, and into the kitchen. No one looked at me. I took an apple out of the refrigerator, walked back, and stood by the table.

"What a delicious looking turkey," I said as I bit the apple.

"It sure is," answered the father with his mouth full of food.

I returned to my room and watched television. Harry's family left soon after dinner.

"Hey, Jean, I have plenty of leftovers. Are you hungry?" asked Harry.

"Yes, Harry, I am hungry, but I would rather starve than eat your parents' leftovers," I said, leaving for Morrison's Cafeteria. As I was eating, I wondered whether or not I would have acted normally at the table with Harry's family.

The following week I took an early flight to Haiti. I wanted to impress my father with my bachelor's degree and job as assistant export manager. Again I traveled with a few gifts, hoping to buy my way into his life.

I dressed in a business suit. I was not nervous this time, because I did not feel like I had to pass inspection. But my mission was the same as before: to be accepted and recognized in name by my father, Philippe.

After going through customs, I took a taxi to 18 Rue Bernard. The same maid answered the door and recognized me.

"No one is home," she said.

I went to Madame Laroche's house. Another family was living there. The next-door neighbor was surprised to see me and said that Madame Laroche had sold the house to send Mademoiselle Marie-Claire to medical school in Mexico. Jérôme had gone to law school in Paris, and Monsieur Laroche had left his wife and *placé* for a younger woman. Jérôme was supporting his mother.

I returned to Philippe's house and greeted him with "Bonjour" and shook his hand.

"Are you still in the army?" he asked.

"No, I left the army five years ago. I graduated from the University of South Florida, and I am working as an assistant VP for an export company," I said. Philippe motioned yes with his head. He seemed ill at ease with me.

"I am here because I would like to get to know you. I want to work with you and travel with you," I said.

"I don't have the time. I am always busy and I don't need help," said Philippe. I felt embarrassed and glued to the floor. For a brief moment I experienced a sinking feeling, similar to a free fall in a nightmare. I heard a car in the driveway. Two young mulatto men in their twenties walked into the living room. They were Philippe's twins. They kissed him on both cheeks.

"Bonjour, Papa," they said, and shook my hand. The twins had met me on my previous trip to Haiti. Philippe pulled out a roll of paper money from his pocket and distributed nearly all of it to the twins.

"Merci, Papa," they said. They had dropped out of school and were living with their mother in Pétionville, a wealthy suburb north of Port-au-Prince.

"We'll see you later, Papa," they said.

"Okay," said Philippe.

"Hey, Bobby, would you like to get together this evening?" said one of the twins.

"Yes, I would like that," I answered.

"I'll pick you up around eight," he said. I was pleased by my brother's invitation. Philippe went to his room and changed his clothes.

"I'll see you later when I get back," he said.

Around eight o'clock in the evening, the twins picked me up in their car. One offered me a cigarette and I declined.

"No thank you, I don't smoke," I said. The twins looked at each other and lit their cigarettes. It was hot and humid that night. The cigarette smoke was making me sick.

"If my brothers and I hit it off, maybe my father will overlook my kinky hair and welcome me into his life. He might even give me his last name—then I'll be somebody," I said to myself.

"We're going to a party, Bobby. I already have a girl waiting for you," said the one driving.

"Oui, merci," I replied, trying to stick my head out of the window to get fresh air.

The car stopped in a dead-end street and the driver turned off the headlights. I was nervous.

"What are we doing on this dark street?" I asked.

"We're waiting for someone," answered the driver twin.

A short while later, someone appeared in the dark, approached the car, handed the driver twin a small paper bag, and vanished.

"You get high, don't you?" asked the passenger twin.

"Sometimes," I answered, feeling let down. As the car began to move, I thought, "If we're caught and arrested, the police will beat me to death and let my brothers go." I stretched and yawned loudly in the backseat.

"I am very tired and sleepy. I had a long flight. I want to skip the party tonight," I said. There was silence. They dropped me off in front of Philippe's house and said good-bye.

"I blew it," I said to myself. I walked in and found Philippe in the living room reading a *Paris-Match*.

"You're back so soon?" he asked.

"I have something to tell you," I said. Philippe lowered the magazine and stared at me.

"What is it?" he asked.

"The boys are using illegal drugs. On the way to the party, they stopped somewhere and made a purchase," I said.

Philippe's face turned angry and he dropped his head.

"I don't use drugs," I added, hoping he would choose me over the twins. He went to his room without saying goodnight.

"What have I done? I should have said nothing," I thought, and went to bed in the room that Madelaine used to occupy. The next morning Philippe was still upset. I told him that I was leaving and he grumbled something. I tipped the maids, took a taxi to the airport, and returned to Tampa.

At work one day, I returned from lunch to find a big chocolate cake with one candle on my desk. On a small table in the corner was a brown paper bag full of paper plates, napkins, and forks. Suddenly I remembered the birth date that was on my passport. I dialed Andrea, the department secretary, and thanked her, feeling undeserving. I carried the cake and the bag to my car and drove home. I placed the cake in the refrigerator and returned to work. At about two o'clock, Andrea walked into my office with the rest of the department's personnel.

"What's going on?" I asked, wondering why everyone was in my office.

"Where's the cake?" asked Andrea.

"What cake?" I asked.

"The cake I put on your desk right after lunch," she said.

"I thought you said it was my cake," I said.

"Yes, it's your cake, but we're here to celebrate your birthday with it. Don't kid around like that now—the joke's over. Where's the cake? We're here for dessert," she said, searching behind my desk.

"Come on now, Jean, let's cut the cake," said José. Embarrassed, I placed my hands over my eyes.

"I took the cake home," I said slowly. Everyone looked at each other and walked out.

"Oh no," I said. I walked over to Andrea's work area. "I am so sorry, Andrea. I didn't know what to do because I never had a birthday before," I explained.

"I don't believe you. Look at you. Your parents put you through college and they never gave you a birthday? You expect me to believe that?" asked Andrea, looking at me from head to foot. I walked back to my office and sat pensively behind my desk. I began to feel uncomfortable around my peers and the secretaries. I thought about killing Florence and myself again.

A month later, I took a week's vacation and decided to drive to New York to confront Florence. I packed a small bag and took off at three o'clock in the morning. I drove all day, stopping only for food, gas, and rest rooms. By late evening, I arrived in New York and spent the night at the home of my high school friend Nicolas.

I learned that Florence had moved out of Lise's house because their relationship had deteriorated. Florence had bought a small two-bedroom house and was living alone.

The next morning after breakfast, I placed my overnight bag in the car and drove to Florence's house. I parked across the street. The house needed repairs and the yard looked neglected. I walked to the front door with my overnight bag. I knocked. Florence opened the door.

"Oh my son, it's you, come in," she said, smiling. She had never referred to me as her son before. Her three front teeth were missing and the left side of her face was darker than the other. Part of her gray kinky hair was visible around the edge of her straight black wig. I followed her in. Her back was bent slightly under her housecoat.

Red faded velour curtains with huge water spots hung unevenly in the dimly lit living room. Cobwebs dangled from the ceiling. On a small glass coffee table was a skull-shaped mug holding three artificial roses. The smell of BenGay and mildew caused my nose to twitch. She stopped in the kitchen. The stove was stained with old particles of food and the sink was full of dirty pots and pans.

"Sit down, my son," she said, knocking two small cockroaches off the table with the back of her hand.

"Roaches are everywhere; I just can't seem to get rid of them," she said. I sat across from her and placed the bag in front of me.

"Would you like some coffee?" she asked.

"No thank you," I said, as tears began to form in my eyes.

"I am glad to see you. I thought you had forgotten all about me," she said. I took a deep breath. I was nervous. "I am not a shoeshine boy," I said. Florence seemed embarrassed. She kept her eyes on the table.

"I came to tell you how much you've hurt me, but I don't know where to start," I continued with quivering lips. Florence opened her mouth to talk.

"Please, don't say anything. It's my turn to talk now. For fifteen years, you prevented me from expressing my wants, my needs, my feelings, and my opinions. Do you remember how you used to pull and pinch my penis and how you used to beat me in my sleep for wetting the rags that served as my bed? I thought you hated me because I have a penis. I tried to cut it off just to please you. You struck me on my eye with the heel of your shoe because I broke a glass. I bled and I could not see with the eye. Look at the scar—I still have it," I said, pointing to the corner of my right eye. "It was the cook who washed my face and took care of me." At that moment tears filled Florence's eyes.

"You let your friends borrow me like I was some kind of human vacuum cleaner. Remember when I was supposed to have my First Communion? I received the sacrament in the army. It was embarrassing telling the priest that my mother didn't want to spend money to buy me clothes and shoes." Tears began to flow from her eyes.

"When your son was about to take me to the police station, I looked at you and you said nothing. If I hadn't run away, the police would have killed me. You nearly killed me when you put a foot on my neck because I lost a dollar. Yes, I *lost* the dollar. I had a hole in my pocket. You used to give more than that to your lover Paul. Where is he now?"

Florence was sobbing. She took a napkin and wiped her eyes. I too took a napkin and wiped my eyes, but the tears kept flowing.

"I was so scared when you made me wash your bloody rags. I had no idea where the blood came from. I thought you were dying. When we moved to the Villards' house, you referred to their children as little darlings, but me, I was extrait caca—a shithead, a little faggot, a shoeshine boy. You used to tell me that my real mother was a dog and I used to believe you."

"Please stop, you're hurting me," interrupted Florence crying.

"I am not finished yet," I yelled, hitting the table with my fist as tears and sweat dripped from my chin.

"You stood by and watched as your friend Yvette forced me down on my knees and pushed my head into a dirty toilet. Where is she now? You celebrated your birthday, your son's birthday, your daughter-in-law's birthday, and your grandchildren's birthdays—but every year you said to me that my birthday was last month. Did you really have to lock me out of the house whenever you spent the day with your friends? You could have taken me with you—I was a good boy. A month ago a lady at work put a cake on my desk to celebrate my birthday. You want to know what I did? I took the cake home to my apartment while no one was looking because I did not know what to do. When I was in the army, every time a soldier passed gas I instinctively said, 'Excuse me.' You know, several times I imagined myself killing you." Florence looked up and stared into my eyes.

"Why don't you kill me and get it over with right now!" exclaimed Florence.

"I should be here with you to take care of you, to take you out to dinner, and to say proudly to all my friends, 'This is my mother.' But I can't because you hurt me so much." I stood up, still sobbing. I slowly unzipped the bag, pulled out my bachelor's degree, and placed it in front of her.

"I am not a shoeshine boy," I said again.

I walked out and closed the door behind me, feeling free, renewed, and vindicated. As I approached my car, I took a deep breath and felt as though I was breathing for the very first time.

19 **I returned to Tampa,** finished my second year at Citrus International, and resigned. I immediately landed a new export job with a smaller company in New York City. My boss was Bill, a tall and slender white man with a strong New York accent. I was to locate foreign buyers and sell them foodstuffs. I soon contacted all of my former European clients and located a customer who wanted to buy a shipment of honey. The supplier, who was in North Carolina, had agreed to our terms over the telephone but insisted on seeing my company's financial statements. I was to fly to North Carolina for a face-to-face meeting with him before the deal could be finalized. I approached Bill and explained the transaction to him.

"White businessmen in North Carolina don't like to do business with blacks. I think I should handle this transaction myself so you won't jeopardize it," said Bill.

"What about my commission?" I asked.

"What about it? Whoever handles a transaction gets the commission," he said boldly. Once again the voice of Alvina Jefferson echoed in my head: "Negroes don't have anything because the white man won't let them." I walked out of his office feeling disgusted, thinking there must be some kind of organized conspiracy by white men to keep blacks financially disadvantaged. The commission on that transaction alone would have equaled my yearly salary of sixteen thousand dollars.

I cleaned out my desk and left the company, taking with me the names of my clients. I returned to my efficiency apartment, which had been rented for me by a white friend because the landlord would not rent to blacks. I packed my car and headed west to California. I wanted to live there because I had heard that Californians were liberal and sophisticated.

Once in Los Angeles, I found it impossible to land an export job. It seemed that businesses preferred any other race to blacks. In desperation I approached a tire shop, and was hired on the spot as a tire mounter for four dollars an hour. The work was backbreaking. The shop manager timed new workers with a stopwatch. Speed was more important than customers' safety. I worked five days a

week with every Thursday and Sunday off. A young black salesman at the shop who happened to be looking for a fourth roommate rented me a room in a house he was renting. During evening
hours, I attended a technical school, taking courses in computer
programming, hoping to land a better job in one of those big
weapons factories.

Early one Thursday morning the telephone rang. It was my boss
at the tire shop. "I wanna see you in my office right now," he said.
I assumed that he wanted me to work overtime. I reported to work
immediately wearing my work clothes. "Don't bother punching in,
you're not working," he snapped. Waiting in his office was a tall
white man in a blue suit, holding a metal case.

"Where were you Tuesday night about ten o'clock?" asked the
manager. His tone of voice made me nervous.

"I was home reading in bed," I said.

"Two of our stores were robbed last night. Do you know anything about it?" he asked.

"No. Like I said, I was home reading in bed," I replied.

"If you didn't do it, you have nothing to worry about. We want
you to take a polygraph—it's company policy," he said.

"I didn't rob your store and I am not taking a polygraph," I
replied nervously.

"You're fired. Hit the road, Jack!" he yelled.

I went to clean out my locker and noticed my name written in a
letter posted on the bulletin board. It said: "Please review with
your staff the attached policies on cash drops. We have had two of
our stores held up and want you all to be aware of the policy on the
cash, checks and credit card drafts to be kept in the cash drawers.
If you have any questions regarding the policy please contact the
credit department. The description of the suspect is as follows:
Black male between the ages of 25 and 30, 5'9" tall, 165 pounds,
alone and armed. This is either Jean or Frank, watch them close." I
am 5'8" and weighed 135 pounds, and Frank was shorter than I.

I took down the letter and left with it in my pocket. After a few
days, I made several copies and went to the Equal Employment
Opportunity Commission, where I filed a wrongful termination
complaint against the shop. Within thirty days, I received a reply

informing me of a scheduled hearing. In the meantime my car was repossessed, my credit was destroyed, and I was evicted from my rented room. I found myself sleeping among the homeless on Venice Beach and eating charity meals at the Hare Krishna compound every afternoon. I was angry and wanted recourse. I felt wronged and abused. I couldn't complain to either the police or the courts—not even city hall, the White House or Congress. Alvina Jefferson was too far away. I had no wife or children to tell. I wanted my frustrations known to the world. I wanted to explode, but the riot in Watts had happened twenty years too soon. I was no longer grateful to white America for my college education and I began to have the same attitude as the black American students at Spring Valley High School.

At the EEOC, the tire company was ordered to make restitution to me. I was offered my job back, but since I had some dignity left in me, I filed a lawsuit against the tire shop instead. After nearly two years of out-of-court negotiations, my white attorney accepted a settlement of thirty thousand dollars, out of which he paid himself about seventeen thousand.

Upon graduation from the technical school, I landed a job as a computer programmer in a large computer service company. Everything was going well and I was trying to forget the past. As at Citrus International, I was the only black in the company besides the janitor.

A beautiful young brunette caught my gaze in the department. I saw her in a fast-food restaurant one day during lunch and asked her permission to share her table. She agreed and we began to have lunch regularly. She and I would meet every Friday afternoon at a local bistro for drinks and dinner. Our friendship became obvious to everyone at work. One Friday afternoon, after I was handed my paycheck, my boss called me into his office.

"I want you to resign because your behavior is not conducive to the image we want to maintain in this company," he said.

"What exactly did I do wrong?" I asked, feeling like my world had been shattered again.

"We're a very conservative-minded company, and your behavior is not compatible with our image—you understand, don't you?" he said, handing me a paper to sign. I walked out without signing it. Early in the morning, I packed my car and headed back to Florida. Once I reached Tampa, I stopped at my alma mater and felt a strong desire to return to class as a young freshman again. I walked into one of the buildings and sat in an empty classroom. The familiar smell seemed to soothe my wounded Haitian soul.

When I returned to Mrs. Jefferson's house, she welcomed me back with open arms. Her three children, several grandchildren, and a few great-grandchildren were on the front porch. Everyone was eager to hear about California. I talked about the incident at the tire shop as well as the one at the computer service company. Mrs. Jefferson's son George reminisced about police brutality, her daughters talked about racist bosses at work, her grandchildren talked about police harassment, and Mrs. Jefferson summarized it all with "They're evil I tell you, the white man is evil," while her great-grandchildren's minds recorded everything that was said for the next generation.

I wanted to take a break and a deep breath before I swam back upstream into the white business world again. I ran into an acquaintance who told me that she was working as a substitute teacher, and I thought I should try subbing for a while. I applied at the Hillsborough County School Board in Tampa and was soon sent to King High School. I entered a ninth-grade history class and immediately fell in love with teaching. The smell of the classroom took me back to Mr. Rabinowitz's history class, and for a brief moment I felt like I was him. The class was integrated, with black students the majority. As I began to speak, a dark-skinned black girl who was not familiar with my Caribbean accent raised her hand. "Are you black?" she asked. I was slightly offended by her question, considering what I had been through because of my skin color.

"Of course I am. You and I may be related," I answered. Suddenly everyone was very attentive. "During the days of slavery, when slave ships dropped off slaves here from Africa, they sometimes continued to the Caribbean to drop off more slaves. It's possible that our distant relatives may have been on one of those ships," I added. Suddenly her eyes and smile lit the room.

Everyone had a question about slaves in the Caribbean. Since their regular teacher didn't leave a lesson plan, I told the class how African slaves in Haiti emancipated themselves, fought the powerful French army, and created the first independent black republic in the Western Hemisphere. But I was too ashamed to tell them that, after independence, affluent blacks and mulattoes reintroduced slavery under the label *restavec*. The black students listened with gleaming eyes as if Toussaint-Louverture and Jean-Jacques Dessalines were their great-uncles. I also wanted to tell them about my life as a restavec in Haiti and in New York, but I didn't for fear that they would taunt me with the word *restavec* in the cafeteria during the lunch period.

Their history textbooks, it seemed, had been written by whites for the benefit of white students. They had been taught that slave masters like George Washington and Thomas Jefferson were their heroes. Slaves who had masterminded insurrections and killed their slave masters in their attempts to free their fellow bondsmen were not mentioned. They had never heard of slaves like Toussaint-Louverture, David Walker, Nat Turner, Denmark Vesey, Gabriel Prosser, and others who had advocated and used violence to overthrow the slave system—they knew only of the nonmilitant blacks like Frederick Douglass, Sojourner Truth, and Martin Luther King Jr.

After class, some of the black students approached me to find out whether I would return the next day to finish the story about Toussaint-Louverture. They were eager to learn the story of people like themselves, not stories about people who used to own their ancestors.

I wanted to teach for three reasons. First, teaching was giving me a chance to be a Mr. Rabinowitz to black American students. Second, school was the only place where I ever felt safe. And third, the thought of going back to the profit-making world was making me feel like a swimmer who was about to dive in murky waters.

I went to the teachers college at the University of South Florida, where an adviser reviewed my transcript and presented me with a list of courses that I needed to take to become a history teacher. After reviewing several history textbooks, I decided to teach French, one of the languages with which I grew up. After I completed all the requirements, I was ready to intern as a student teacher. The white middle-aged woman who was in charge of placing interns with high school teachers had difficulty finding me a placement in Hillsborough County. After nearly two months of waiting, I was getting impatient. I went back to the teachers college and demanded a refund.

"I can't find a high school in Hillsborough County that will accept you. Will you consider going to another county?" she asked me.

"Yes, I will, but I don't want to travel very far," I replied.

She promised to call me as soon as she found a placement.

On a Friday afternoon, the telephone rang. It was the woman at the teachers college. She told me to report to Hudson High School in Pasco County, just over an hour's drive away, and that Ms. Cynthia Nassano had agreed to take me as an intern. I was not too excited about going to a county where Klan activities were constantly in the news, but I had no other choice.

I immediately telephoned Ms. Nassano to confirm the information.

Monday morning I reported to Hudson High School and waited nervously in the front office. Soon I was greeted with a handshake and a warm smile by a young brunette. I followed her to the teachers' lounge, where she introduced me to a group of white teachers. The bell rang and I followed her again, to a classroom that was soon filled with white students. They looked at me with curiosity in their eyes. Ms. Nassano introduced me to the class as a student teacher. As subsequent classes came in, I noticed that there were no black students. During the lunch period, I walked through the cafeteria looking for black students as everyone seemed to stare at me like I was lost. I noticed an African face, but it belonged to a middle-aged lady who was holding a mop. There were no African American students in the school.

Ms. Nassano and I developed a fast friendship. She thought I was efficient and intelligent. Sometimes I brought her fresh donuts for breakfast to show my appreciation, not realizing that she was falling in love with me, a former child restavec.

"I can't believe I have to drive this far for my internship while there are many schools in Hillsborough County," I said.

"The woman who called me asked if I would be willing to accept an intern. She told me your name and said, 'He's black.' I said, 'So, what difference does it make?' Then she said, 'That might matter to some people.' She might have told every French teacher in Hillsborough County that you were black," explained Ms. Nassano. I began to wonder why black parents were sending their black children to be educated by racist teachers, not realizing that they had no other choice.

By the time I completed my internship at Hudson High, my friendship with Ms. Nassano had become more than just amicable. Since she was relocating to Ohio, she recommended me to the principal as her replacement. I was hired to replace her the following school year.

As the only black member on the staff, I felt genuinely welcome. My colleagues went out of their way to make me feel comfortable. My students were white except for Udey, a dark-skinned eleventh-grade boy from India. In my opinion, he was the brightest student in the school. His father was a medical doctor in the community. On the surface, Udey was accepted by his peers. He was well liked by the girls, who considered him just a "friend" for his own protection.

As I was walking past a group of boys one morning near the cafeteria, I heard, "Hey, nigger" shouted at me. When I turned around, everyone was quiet. As I continued on my way to class, they shouted "Nigger" at me again. Suddenly I thought about the story Alvina Jefferson had told me about the little white girl who was following and staring at her. I wanted to say something back to the boys, but somehow I felt that teachers should be the ultimate role models for any race of students. And I also knew that any type of retaliation would have resulted in my immediate dismissal. I ignored the boys and continued to my destination, but I felt discouraged. I had lost my wind to teach my last two classes.

One day while grading a stack of papers, I noticed several boys' papers with the initials KKK in large letters on the very first line. I lectured the class on the cowardliness of the KKK. To my surprise, they stopped adding the initials except for one boy, who told me that I was infringing upon his freedom of expression. I wrote on his paper: "I have the right not to be insulted." I also stopped grading his work. When he realized that, he stopped the behavior.

Before the school year ended, I walked past the same group of boys near the cafeteria. I made a sudden turn when I reached the point where I usually heard "nigger" shouted at me and saw the word coming out of the culprit's mouth. I found out his name and reported him to the office. His father, who was called in for a conference, swore that he didn't know where his son had learned to use the word. Nevertheless, he was given a five-day out-of-school suspension.

My experiences with the white students at Hudson High completed the Americanization of my black Haitian soul. I am now a true American black man despite my Caribbean accent.

Cindy and I continued our relationship despite the distance that separated us. We wrote each other often, and I visited her during four-day weekends and spring break. At the end of the school year, I resigned my position and moved to Cincinnati, Ohio, a very conservative city, to join Cindy. Even today, some people in Cincinnati still decorate their front lawn with a lawn jockey, a small statue of an African slave in a red jacket and white trousers holding a metal ring, although Ohio was never a slave state. Or maybe it's an unconscious desire to be a plantation owner, to have enough wealth to own a well-dressed stable boy for the purpose of greeting guests at the gate and handling their surreys.

I asked a black mailman and a black gas meter reader how they felt when they went to these homes every day. "It makes my blood boil," replied the mailman with anger in his voice.

"I don't like it. I think it's offensive, but there's nothing I can do about it," replied the meter reader.

I wanted to marry Cindy Nassano and I was not too concerned about her being white. I loved her very much because she believed in me and thought I was special, even after I told her about my life as a former slave child, living in absolute poverty in Haiti, the poorest country in the Western Hemisphere.

I was more concerned about not having my own relatives at our wedding than being the only black person in it. One of Cindy's brothers, whom I had met two years earlier, stood by my side as my best man. I was uncomfortable, feeling like I had just crawled out from under a rock.

After the wedding I found myself very uncomfortable, being both husband and stepfather. Cindy had a four-year-old daughter named Katrina. It seemed as though I was in a play for which I knew neither my lines nor my position in any of the scenes. During meals I sometimes locked myself in a closet and refused to come out. Other times I would eat alone in the kitchen where I was more at ease, as if I had become a child restavec once again.

I sabotaged the birthdays Cindy planned for me by cutting the cake and leaving the house before the occasion.

The nightmares began coming back. Almost every night I was screaming and fighting a giant monster which caused me to kick and punch Cindy. I would wake up at the sound of her voice calling my name from where she sat at the very edge of the bed: "Jean, wake up, honey."

Cindy insisted that I return to counseling or else. I was reluctant to do so because I didn't want to retell the horror of my childhood to a new psychiatrist. But the pain in her face convinced me otherwise.

During the sessions, Cindy cried more than I did, shaking her head in disbelief, listening attentively to the horror that is now very much a part of her life. After each visit, I slept on a sleeping bag in the closet to avoid hurting her and to hide from the monsters of my past. The sessions provided some relief but they were not a cure.

It seems that many people are uncomfortable and suspicious when they see blacks and whites walking together in American society. Once I took Katrina, my four-year-old blond stepdaughter, with me to the grocery store to purchase a gallon of milk. She began to cry because I wouldn't buy candy for her. As I carried her out to the car, a concerned citizen took my license plate number, called the police, and reported that a white child was being kidnapped by a black man. Before I reached my house, the police had been there, questioning my Cindy to make sure that her daughter had not in fact been abducted.

On another occasion, I went to pick Katrina up from preschool for the very first time. I entered the large room in the basement

of a church and was greeted by a young brunette about twenty
years old.

"I am here to pick up my stepdaughter Katrina," I informed the
young woman.

"The children are napping right now. I'll go get her," she said
smilingly, and disappeared into another room. Soon she returned
with the only black child in her care and placed her in my arms.

"This is not my daughter. Katrina is blond," I said, looking at
the sleeping dark-skinned child.

"Oops!" she said, taking back the child and disappearing again.
She returned empty-handed about five minutes later.

"May I see some ID?" she asked. I handed her my driver's license
which she verified against Katrina's file, making sure that I was indeed authorized to pick her up.

I was hired by the Cincinnati Public Schools for the 1988–1989
school year to teach French and social studies in a middle school. I
was eager to be a Mr. Rabinowitz in the lives of some black children.

My assigned school was located in a run-down black neighborhood. When I entered the building, I was in awe. The large reception room was freshly painted and the walls were decorated with
the flags of almost every nation on earth. I had the feeling that I
was walking into the United Nations building in New York, although I had never been there. When the school buses began to ar-
rive, I noticed that nearly all the children being unloaded were
black. Then I saw a great many white children being driven to
school by their parents.

I was to teach four classes of sixth-grade world history and
two classes of seventh-grade Ohio studies. In two of my sixth-
grade classes, all the children were white except for two blacks. In
all classes the white students were well prepared. They did their
homework regularly and everything else that was expected of
them. The black students, however, were the complete opposite
except for a handful. They fought in the hallways, shouted profan-
ity, called each other "nigga," and spent less time in the classrooms
than their white peers. They were constantly on their way to the
bathroom or waiting in the office to see the assistant principal.

I soon learned that the school district was under court order to desegregate. The decorations, the name change from Warner Middle School to Foreign Language Academy, and the total immersion in foreign language programs were all designed to attract white middle-class students. While the building was desegregated, most of the classrooms were not. And while many black parents actually believed that their children would get a better education if they sat next to whites, some white parents were requesting that their children be placed in classes that had few or no black students.

Every Friday afternoon, a group of white teachers invited me to join them at a local bistro for happy hour. They told me that I was different from other blacks. We would discuss the principal's lack of leadership and her refusal to discipline black children. The few black teachers on the staff referred to me as a "sellout" and "one of them."

I decided to become Mr. Rabinowitz to three black students who caught my attention. I thought they were tractable and had great potential. One was a thirteen-year-old blind girl named Tamika who reminded me of Anita, my childhood restavec friend in Haiti. She tried to show her independence by keeping to herself. I decided to eat lunch with her every day in the cafeteria to get to know her. After having lunch with me three times, she told her mother that I was "hitting" on her and that I wanted to have sex with her. I was soon ordered to stay away from Tamika.

The second student was Deandre, a fourteen-year-old boy. I called his house one evening because I hadn't seen him in two weeks. His mother told me that she had decided to keep him home because he had a "leakage" problem. He once brought me a note from his mother that read: "Deandre could not do his homework last night because the water main in our neighborhood broke."

Then there was Marcus, a high-spirited, intelligent, yet lazy sixth grader with very dark skin. I taught the class standing next to him every day, looking over his shoulder to make sure he was taking notes. One day I was called into the principal's office for a conference with Marcus's mother. The principal, a black woman, was sitting behind her desk like a queen on her throne. Marcus's mother was sitting in front of the principal's desk. I sat in a chair away from Marcus's mother.

"This is Marcus's mother, Mrs. Booker. She wants to talk to you about her son in your sixth-grade class," said the principal.

"Marcus told me that you're making his life miserable and that you stand next to him in class, and you look over his shoulder, and you don't do that to the white boys in your class," said Mrs. Booker.

"Marcus needs constant attention. To have a good class, I have to stand next to him," I explained.

"Marcus also told me that when the white boys misbehave, you don't do anything about it. It seems to me that you favor white children over black children. I listen to you, you don't sound like a black man. You look black, but you ain't black," said Mrs. Booker. I looked at her and smiled nervously.

"You don't understand black children, do you, Mr. Cadet?" asked the principal.

"Yes, I do understand black children," I said.

"I don't think you do," answered Mrs. Booker. Each time I tried to talk about Marcus's behavior, I was interrupted and lectured about my lack of blackness. After the meeting, I walked out thinking about my white father who wanted nothing to do with me because I was born black with kinky hair. Although I feel neither black nor white, I am as American as a black man from the Deep South, with enough emotional battle scars to earn me a dozen Purple Hearts.

I concluded that it is easier to be a Mr. Rabinowitz to white students than to black students, because black students tend to think of education as a "white thing."

After the year ended, I transferred to another school. I continued teaching at the high school level while I worked on my master's degree at the University of Cincinnati.

One day in April 1990, a dozen red roses and a card were delivered to my classroom at the high school where I was teaching. My first reaction was that the delivery person must have had the wrong room. "Are you sure it's for me?" I asked. The card was addressed to me. As I opened it, I quickly recognized Cindy's hand-writing. It was her way of announcing to me that she was pregnant. I loved her before, but now I was beginning to feel safe with her— as if I were allowing her to pack my parachute while I watched with one eye open.

That particular week, two of my professors suggested that I work toward my Ph.D. I came home feeling like I was walking on air and told that to Cindy. "I think you should do it," she replied in a supportive tone.

When Cindy's water broke on the morning of January 6, 1991, I drove her to the hospital and stayed with her in the delivery room. During labor, I held her hands and assisted her with the breathing techniques we had learned in childbirth classes. As the baby was being born, the emptiness that I'd always felt in my chest was slowly filled. My heart was no longer a stone in the middle of a cold and empty cave. After the delivery, the nurse plopped a beau-tiful baby boy in my arms. I looked in his eyes and saw something that reminded me of Blanc Philippe. Inside me was an explosion of contentment that vibrated all the way up to the shores of my eyes.

That spring, the diploma for my master's degree arrived in the mail as I played with Adam, my son.

AFTERWORD

Although the birth of Adam filled the void in my chest, I still became clinically depressed at times, especially during holidays when everyone I knew seemed to be on the way to reconnect with family members. When Adam's grandmother, grandfather, aunt, and uncles visited us, I felt like a thing that had just crawled out from under a rock because I couldn't bring myself to make any reference to my family, the people who raised me. As I watched Adam in the arms of his grandma, reaching for her smiling face, I felt like the silent victim of a rape. Then I realized that Adam too was a victim, a casualty of restavec servitude. Had my former country abolished all forms of slavery, Florence's treatment of me would have never been socially condoned. Perhaps she would have treated me like a son, Denis would have considered me a brother, and Adam would have enjoyed having another grandmother and an uncle on my side of the family.

Restavec slavery is wrong. It is the worst crime imaginable, because the victims are incapable of resisting their adult predators. It is a crime against nature as well, because the child's very rights to life—to belong, to grow, to smile, to love, to feel, to learn, and to be a child—are denied, by those whose ancestors were slaves themselves.